Key to Freedom

*The Seven-Step Model
to Triumph Over Trauma*

Dr Natalie Green

First published by Busybird Publishing 2017
Copyright © 2017 Dr Natalie Green

ISBN
Print: 978-1-925585-61-2
Ebook: 978-1-925585-62-9

Dr Natalie Green has asserted her right under the Copyright, Designs and Patents Act 1988 to be identified as the author of this work. The information in this book is based on the author's experiences and opinions. The publisher specifically disclaims responsibility for any adverse consequences, which may result from use of the information contained herein. Permission to use information has been sought by the author. Any breaches will be rectified in further editions of the book.

All rights reserved. No part of this publication may be reproduced, stored in or introduced into a retrieval system, or transmitted in any form, or by any means (electronic, mechanical, photocopying, recording or otherwise) without the prior written permission of the author. Any person who does any unauthorised act in relation to this publication may be liable to criminal prosecution and civil claims for damages. Enquiries should be made through the publisher.

Cover image: Kev Howlett
Cover design: Busybird Publishing
Layout and typesetting: Busybird Publishing
Editor: Susan Pierotti

Busybird Publishing
2/118 Para Road
Montmorency, Victoria
Australia 3094
www.busybird.com.au

Dedication

To my amazing family – Warren, my loving husband who encourages me constantly, and my wonderful children, Alex and Maddie, who've taught me so much and inspire me every day – thank you for having been by my side throughout it all, supporting me unconditionally and teaching me love, compassion and, most of all, how to live life to the full every day.

To my Mum who instilled commitment, dedication and above all else, a determination never to give up or quit despite life's twists and turns.

To my mentors and teachers along the way (and there have been many) who've nurtured me, challenged me and most of all, believed in me and taught me that it's okay to shine.

To all of you who read this book, this is for every one of you who are brave enough to step up and overcome your pain. Let this be the diamond that you can cut for yourself, polish and allow it to help you shine as brightly as you desire and to create the person that you were always destined to be.

Here's to your success!

Contents

Introduction	i
Chapter 1 – Staying Stuck	1
Chapter 2 – Breaking Moulds	11
Chapter 3 – Transformational Model (Seven Steps)	19
Chapter 4 – Trauma Unlocked	27
Chapter 5 – The Awakening	37
Chapter 6 – Finding Courage	47
Chapter 7 - Letting Go	53
Chapter 8 – Pain Relief	63
Chapter 9 – Begin Again	73
Chapter 10 – Future Design	79
Chapter 11 – Newfound Freedom	87
Chapter 12 – New Normal	95
Afterword	105
Appendix 1	
Symptom Checklist	109
Appendix 2	
Life Change Index Scale (The Stress Test)	112
Appendix 3	
Date Stamping Process	115
Appendix 4	
Negative Energy Release and Permission to Move Forward Process	117
Appendix 5	
Self-Care Practices	119
Appendix 6	
The Negative Emotions Hierarchy	121
References	123
About The Author	125
'Transform Your Life' Online Course	127
Dr Natalie Green as a guest speaker	129
ABS Certification	131

Introduction

"If you think you can, you will. If you think you can't, you won't and if you think you are beaten, you are."
Sandra Ayers

For years I've worked with people who have experienced trauma. It never ceases to amaze me how often in the beginning they downplay their trauma or minimise it, as they don't believe they 'deserve' to be taking up my time as 'it wasn't that bad'. Or they don't want to be seen as weak or to feel vulnerable.

This saddens me; it really does.

Being traumatised does *not* mean that you had to witness someone die, or see or experience something so horrific you could never repeat it to anyone. No.

Psychological distress following exposure to a traumatic or stressful event is quite variable.

Thankfully, progress has been made from a clinically diagnostic perspective. In the latest Diagnostic and Statistical Manual of Mental Disorders (the 'bible' for diagnosing disorders), the DSM-V, disorders relating to trauma have now been grouped under a separate category, 'Trauma and Stressor-Related Disorders'. This recognises that while some people will exhibit anxiety and fear-based symptoms, others will demonstrate prominent anhedonic (i.e. the inability to experience pleasure in activities you used to enjoy) and dysphoric (i.e. a profound state of unease or dissatisfaction) symptoms, externalising their anger and aggressive symptoms or even dissociative symptoms.

What that simply means is that trauma won't just show itself as anxiety and fear, but instead it can also present itself as an inability to feel anything much at all, or a general dissatisfaction with life right through to anger and aggressive behaviours.

While I've been a psychologist/clinical psychologist for twenty-seven years, the majority of those years I've worked with people in the area of trauma, with people who've suffered a loss or life-changing experience. They have felt stuck, had their life on hold, been treading water; ultimately they've reached a point where they've had enough.

I've done an undergraduate degree in psychology, a master's degree in rehabilitation counselling and a doctorate in clinical and health psychology by coursework. I now work more in the area of coaching and motivation and mentoring. I've attended conferences all around the world and attended workshops and keynote speeches. I've gathered so much information from all of these sources and learnt so much from applying all that I've learnt with my thousands of clients.

Yet despite all of this, I was so sick of seeing people suffering for years, despite providing them the recognised treatments of choice. It was so hard for me to continue to see their pain as they were reliving their experiences, their emotions, their pain and fears and I knew that there simply had to be another way.

So I started putting together my own process utilising an

eclectic mix of elements from a number of different respected and well known (and some not so well-known) therapies. I tested them with a broad range of people presenting with multiple issues and I have developed a model that I have now named the Accelerated Breakthrough Strategies (ABS) model.

It's actually not just a model, it's a system, a seven-step system that can be put into practice with every client I've seen. It's individualised for each client, but it still follows the seven-step process. It could be a police officer who has experienced multiple complex traumas over the years in their role; a domestic violence victim who has endured untold violence and physical and emotional abuse who needs to let go of the trauma attached to this experience, so that they can work through the damage that has been done to re-create the person and the life that they want for themselves again; a sexual assault victim who has suffered untold trauma; or someone who has experienced the loss of a child, a partner, or even someone who has experienced the loss of a relationship. They simply can't move forward, they're stuck and they're not sure really why.

This model has worked for all these people. What I love about it is that it's efficient, it's effective and it gets results. By working through the seven steps in as little as three sessions, you can process traumas without actually needing to talk about it, without reliving the entire experience and bringing up all the negative emotions that keep you stuck in it as we process it. The ABS system enables you to move through the issue so that you can let go of the part of the trauma that has kept you stuck, complete the process and feel empowered enough to create your identity from scratch, or take the components of who you are that you want to maintain, combined with the learnings that you have experienced from the trauma and to create the lifestyle you actually want.

I've worked with people who have experienced the most intense horrific experiences you could ever begin to imagine. I was working for a year in Port Arthur after the massacre, right at the coal face, with people who'd experienced the most horrendous of traumas imaginable. I saw first-hand the impact of these traumatic events across all areas of their life, and while we did the absolute best we could at the time, I wish I had known about this process back then as it could have helped even more.

I then went on to work with hundreds of people who were in a mine when it collapsed in central west NSW. Even though the majority escaped with their lives, some of their colleagues' lives were lost. I worked for a year with these people, helping them recover from their untold traumas, and witnessed first-hand the complete impact this trauma had across all areas of their lives. I provided them with what I believed to be the best practice at the time.

However, knowing what I know now, there really is another way, a way that is more efficient, more effective and gets permanent results and the outcome that they are wanting all along.

Unfortunately, six years ago, I had complex reconstructive surgery on my ankle, which unluckily resulted in a significant life-threatening infection and sepsis. I faced my own morbidity. This led to an eight-month period of recovery and untold additional trauma, much of which is best left for another book.

So I write this to let you know that no-one is immune to trauma and distressing events, information and experiences, and to encourage you *not* to minimise your experience of trauma or distress. Acknowledge that if you are demonstrating anxiety, fear, anhedonia, dysphoria or agitation or anger, please be honest with yourself; ask yourself where it has really come from, and what could actually be going on and actively seek help so you can let the negative emotions go and live the life you want again.

This personal experience also fuelled my quest to make it easier for my clients, and also to find a solution that meant when you were traumatised, you didn't have to continue to suffer, reliving and re-experiencing and being re-traumatised in order to move through and get the outcome that you desired.

Now I'm on a mission to get my ABS model out to as many people as I possibly can, people who have been traumatised themselves, family members who have experienced the impact of this trauma on a daily basis, and therapists, clinicians, and professionals who work with people who are traumatised so as they too, can be trained in the ABS model from a therapeutic standpoint, so that they can deliver the deeper transformations that the one-on-one therapy can provide through the key stages of the ABS model to make a real difference, to change lives and end countless amounts of suffering as quickly and as effectively as possible.

Converting a one-to-one model that works really well in treatment sessions with a trained professional into a book has been far more challenging than I had anticipated and, as we know, the deepest transformations still come with the one-to-one experience. However I am confident that this self-help book will be a great introduction to empowering people to understand why they are stuck, where they are stuck, and to allow them to let go of a lot of the issues and emotional baggage that has been causing them harm. When you follow the model step by step to completion, this will allow you to create the person you choose to be and to focus on living the life you desire.

Thank you for joining me on this journey and for investing in this book and most of all for investing in yourself, in implementing a solution that will allow you to let go of the pain that is keeping you stuck and allow you to create the future for you and for the significant people in your life, that you truly deserve.

Chapter 1
Staying Stuck

"Growth is painful. Change is painful. But, nothing is as painful as staying stuck where you do not belong."
N.R. Narayana Murthy

We really are funny creatures, us human beings, aren't we? Ideally, we want to experience positive feelings and more actively seek out pleasure and pleasurable experiences. However, what I've noticed from my years and years of working with clients is that they come to me in a significant amount of pain. Often these people have been in pain for long periods of time and they seem pretty entrenched, even set in their ways. They would tell me that they wanted to change and yet their behaviour would tell me something the complete opposite.

We would work on things with all the intentions of making the changes and them taking the action, but they would then come back and nothing had changed or they'd started to make the change, they noticed some improvement and then they'd go back to the behaviours that had created the difficulties in the first place. What I'd noted was that even though they said they didn't want the pain, they often actively sought out even more of the pain.

As human beings, we have a sense of identity, a sense of purpose, a real feel for who we are. It is made up of beliefs, and often our beliefs are instilled from a very young age, learnt from our experiences and picked up from the people around us. Of course these beliefs can be altered when we experience the inevitable trials and tribulations of this thing we call life.

As well as identity and beliefs, we have values. Values are our principles and standards of behaviour, which we judge to be important in life and meaningful to us. They're often known as moral principles or ethics and they serve as a compass for our life. We do not always have conscious awareness of them – rather, they can be at an unconscious level – but we just 'know' they are meaningful for us.

When we make sense of information that comes through to us from the world around us, we have to take it in from an external source and then 'filter' it through various levels internally. These levels include our attitudes, our beliefs, our values, meta-programs (these are the mental processes or shortcuts that direct your decisions, behaviours, actions and interactions with others) and also our memories and experiences. What we know is that these internal filters can delete, distort and generalise the information that comes in before we make sense of it in our own way. So of course we can all experience the exact same event or environment but every human being will have their own filtration process happening and make their experience of that event have different meaning because of these internal filters.

This is never more evident than in the case of trauma. People can experience the exact same event, see the exact same things, be at the same degree of risk, yet have completely different stories to tell and report totally different impacts on their life.

Knowing how this model of communication works makes a huge difference; when we understand these and know all of this happens at an internal (mainly) unconscious level, we can begin to understand that if we want to behave differently, we can target specific components of our internal filter systems, bring them into more conscious awareness and change our behaviour, and subsequently the outcome!

This model of explanation comes predominantly from the field of Neuro Linguistic Programming (NLP) and was developed by Tad James and Wyatt Woodsmall (1988) based on the work of Richard Bandler and John Grinder (1975) and also draws heavily on concepts from the field of cognitive psychology and the ground-breaking work of linguistic analysts Alfred Korzybski (1933) and Naom Chomsky (1964).

This model explains how we take information from the outside world directly into our own neurology and we filter it. This in turn impacts our thoughts, feelings and behaviours.

How We Interpret Information

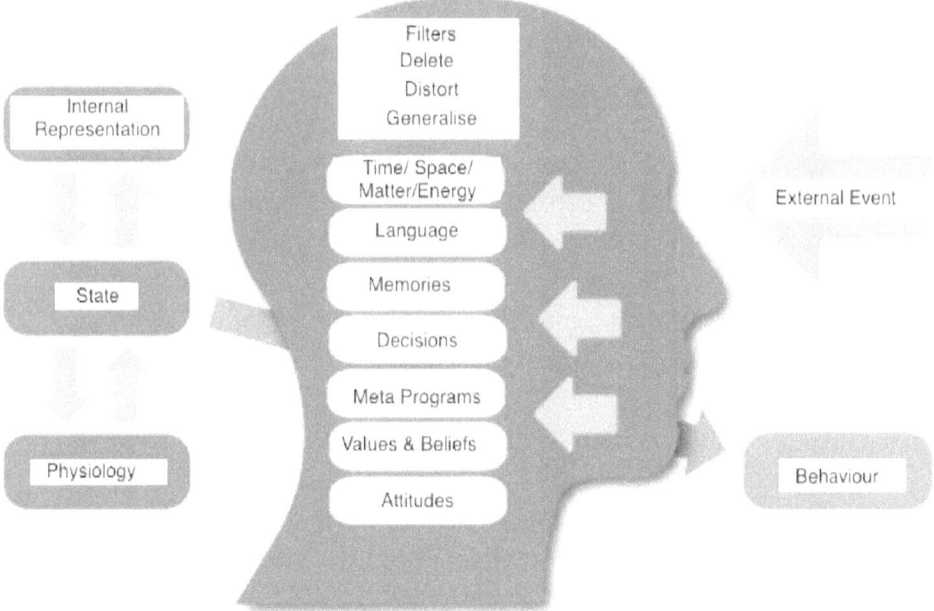

Our filters are unique to each of us and vary from deeply unconscious processes to more conscious ones. It is important to understand exactly what filters we apply to all the information we take in, as when we recognise our behaviour is less than desired or not getting us the outcome we really want, we can target one of these filters at a time and attempt to make some tweaks to alter our outcome so we are more likely to get the outcomes we are truly wanting.

What I see is that even though as humans we might ultimately seek pleasure, so often we make choices to stay stuck in our pain. "Why on Earth would we choose to do that?" you might ask. Well, there are many reasons that someone would choose to stay stuck, even though they know that it creates discomfort.

It can also serve to keep you safe. You know the old saying that 'it's better the devil you know'. Well, often for many people, it is that fear of the unknown that holds them back; it's easier to stay stuck in what you know, and what you've accepted as your current level of functioning and behaviour than it is to change, because you simply don't know what that change will bring for you, and that could be even more frightening for you.

Often what I see with people who've experienced trauma or have issues that are holding them back, or that are creating significant pain, is this fear of wondering what on earth they will do without this in their life. It's often become ingrained, a part of their identity, and there's a fear of wondering what on earth will happen and who they will be without this in their life.

Take, for example, a client I had; let's call her Mary. She said that she couldn't stand things any longer; she was severely depressed, she was crying all the time, she disconnected from everyone, and she was in a domestic violence relationship.

Her partner didn't know she'd come to see me. She knew that what was going on was unhealthy, but she also said to me that it was easier to stay with her partner because 'at least she knew what to expect'. When he would fly into his rages, she knew what would trigger him, when she needed to take cover and how to keep the children safe by taking the beating herself.

Mary's identity and sense of self had been so quashed in this relationship, she had lost sight of who she was, her beliefs were unhelpful, and she knew she wasn't safe, but she felt she deserved what was happening. She'd made the choice that she needed to put up with the consequences. Even though her pain was horrendous, she felt that it was easier to stay there and put up with it as the fear of being all alone and wondering how she would cope with her kids on her own was overwhelming for her.

Yet a big part of her knew that she'd had enough.

So she started working on her trauma and her sense of self, utilising the ABS system. She worked through all seven steps of the system and ultimately managed to leave her relationship, establish herself initially in a safe house, and keep her children safe, put in place the necessary arrangements legally, take a stand for herself and her children and eventually rebuild her sense of identity and create a new life for herself. She's now a single mum raising two children who are safe and she is able to recognise that things can be okay again.

Of course during our sessions, we had to do quite a bit of work on assisting Mary to understand what was in it for her to change and get her focused on the positive outcome, despite not knowing how things would turn out and her having a strong fear of the unknown and finding the uncertainty of this very stressful.

What we often see with people who are trapped by their trauma, who feel stuck and restricted because of the things that have happened in their lives, is that they engage in a lot of self-protective behaviour; in particular, that of shutting off their emotions, because it's simply too hard for them to feel such intense emotions. They disconnect, they disengage and at times they even disassociate. It's as if life goes on around them and they don't have to engage, nor feel what is going on about them and then they can feel 'safe' again.

This is particularly true with some police officers and emergency services workers I've worked with, where they've witnessed so many traumatic incidents, they've experienced so much pain, it's become unbearable and the only way to continue without falling apart themselves has been to numb themselves, to stop processing the emotions and cut themselves off so they're no longer attached.

But in doing so, of course, the consequences are that while they're no longer attached to the traumatic stuff that's causing their pain, they are also detached from the people around them, their relationships suffer with those who they love, they distance themselves, they don't communicate and if they do, then they tend to communicate more with like-minded people, their fellow peers, police officers, and emergency workers who they perceive know exactly what they are going through.

They engage in a 'debrief' over a beer at the pub in order to avoid talking about how they really feel about what's going on. While in many ways this has been quite productive and it has served them well to date, ultimately it is not resourceful in the long term, as often what they learn is they have unknowingly in the process let go of all the things that mattered in their lives – the people, the relationships, the careers, the enjoyment and the positive emotions – by disconnecting and disengaging from the negative emotions.

Chapter 1 – Staying Stuck

By working with hundreds of police officers over the years we've utilised the ABS system with many of them one on one to assist them in letting go of the traumatic memories and experiences, and the emotions attached to them, and to allow them to reconnect with their feelings again. We have done this in a safe and gradual way, letting go of the trauma, the experiences and engaging through the whole seven-step ABS process so they can re-engage with the people that matter to them and re-create the person they want to be. Yes, they tend to be different from the person they were before, but a newer improved version of themselves who have taken on the learnings taught to them from the traumas they have experienced.

What we also know is that there are many people who have been through traumatic experiences or grief and loss, and no matter what the issue, it's likely left them with negative emotions and baggage that they feel is keeping them stuck in many of the ways that we've talked about.

A lot of the time the people I see will have already presented to a doctor or a psychiatrist and they may have been medicated. While this has assisted in allowing them to get some sleep or to calm down, if they've been prescribed something such as valium to reduce their anxiety, they may also be prescribed anti-depressants that serve at times to assist, but really it's just relieving the symptoms and not addressing the underlying cause.

Yes, of course it's okay and can be helpful to be medicated – at times it's absolutely necessary – but it's also really important to understand the impact of the medication and be prepared to allow yourself to explore who you are underneath the medication and gradually reveal the new you and who you want to be through working with the ABS process and letting go of the stuff that's holding you back and keeping you stuck.

One of the other things I've noticed, through the thousands of people I've seen who have presented with trauma or who have experienced negative, destructive emotions as a result of what they've experienced in their lives, is that they continue to go over and over things in their minds, despite them saying they are 'just wanting to shut it out'.

I explain to them that the easiest way I can describe it is to think about our brain as if it is made up of lots of little boxes, lots of little compartments; all the memories and all the experiences we have in our life are all inside those little boxes and that memory network is connected via lots of what we call neural pathways. Everything is ingrained and imprinted on us and while we may not remember everything that's happened in our lives, it will be put inside in a little box in our brain with an emotion attached to it via a memory, a smell, a thought, or a feeling.

It will have been put inside its own little box and when you experience something traumatic and your fight, flight or freeze response is triggered, your adrenalin is increased, you're on edge and scanning your environment in fear, you often tend not to sleep that night and sometimes for many nights afterwards.

What we also know is that sleep is when you process the things that have happened in your life. Whenever you go to sleep you will process what's happened during the day. You work through it, and you attach whatever you need to attach to it to make sense of it, using the filter system I mentioned earlier and then you put it in a box and you close the lid.

All of this is done unconsciously, you're not aware of it, but what we know is that after some sort of trauma, you're not getting sleep at the levels that you normally need due to the trauma response and the extra adrenalin that is produced in our bodies. You don't get to fully process what has happened during the day, so you put it in one of the boxes and close the lid. But it's stuck and it hasn't been fully processed through the usual memory network. It has then attached itself to another memory, another feeling, another thought, another smell, another something, that's associated with something else and it can pop up at any time. The lid on the box doesn't stay closed.

This is how trauma shows itself. What we know is that the ABS system helps people process their trauma, their negative emotions, their negative energies, to let it go and engage in a process of forgiveness so that they can go through the entire seven steps, healing themselves, creating the life and the person that they desire to be, once and for all.

You will see in *Appendix 1* a list of many symptoms that clients present with when they come to see me. What I want you to do is cast your eyes over all of these symptoms. If you recognise many of these symptoms are cropping up for you or you believe you're repeating patterns of unhelpful behaviours that are keeping you stuck, then you are in the right place.

This book is for you and I invite you to come on the journey of self-discovery and give yourself the gift of letting go of all the emotional baggage that is keeping you stuck. Join us on a journey to create the person that you are destined to be.

I invite you to uncover the diamond in the rough, polish it up and let it not only shine, but shine brightly for all the world to see.

Chapter 2
Breaking Moulds

"If you do what you've always done, you'll get what you've always gotten."
Tony Robbins

As I've already mentioned, I've worked with people in counselling, coaching and mentoring roles for twenty-seven years now. And I absolutely love what I do. I've done ten years of university training and achieved three separate degrees, two further years in training under supervision and twenty-seven years of face-to-face treatment.

Thankfully, I pride myself on being engaged, constantly learning and always striving for further education. On top of all the years of formal university training, there have also been course after course, conference after conference, in order to stay across the latest treatments, the latest approaches and most effective strategies to get results for my clients.

But to be honest, absolutely nothing, no amount of theory or training or practical work could have prepared me for the level of trauma and absolute despair that I faced with the Port Arthur massacre. This was closely followed by a far lesser known but very distressing disaster, the collapse of the North Parkes Mine. However, it was through these major events in particular that I got to see first-hand what worked and what didn't and what the lasting impact of trauma really was in reality.

Then through my private practice, for sixteen years I've continually worked with police officers, emergency service workers, sexual assault victims and people with significant posttraumatic stress disorder, trauma responses and considerable whole-person and whole-of-life impacts.

For years I used the models I was trained in, evidence-based best practice. I used Cognitive Behaviour Therapy (CBT) and then I did further training in EMDR (Eye Movement Desensitisation and Reprocessing). I watched demonstrations on EFT, I went to conferences in the United States with the leading gurus in the field who presented keynotes and delivered workshops and I attended them all, like a sponge, and kept working with clients, getting results, all but slowly – far too slowly for my liking.

I then discovered the world of coaching. As I was finding that I was getting really frustrated with all the 'standard' trainings I was doing, focusing on the problem rather than the solution which seemed illogical to me. I wanted to focus on moving forward, finding solutions, rather than having people go over and over the issues and the problems that were the root of their pain and suffering and keeping them stuck. This journey into the world of coaching led to further training and the discovery (for me) of the field of Neuro-Linguistic Programming (NLP). This opened my eyes to a whole new world, a world I hadn't known existed. There's a lot of negative information attached to this field as many people have unfortunately misused or misunderstood the tools that they had been given.

However, as I had done throughout my years, I kept collecting all the information I was trained in. I worked with clients, trialling bits and pieces from varying methodologies, until I noticed that I was getting results with various people that were so much quicker than I'd ever been able to do before. And what's better was that the process that I was using required that they actually didn't have to talk about what had happened to them, what they'd witnessed or what they'd experienced.

To make it even better, they were moving through the process quickly and efficiently. I started to notice that, when they'd turn up for their next session, they even looked different. I know it sounds weird, but it was like they had let go of whatever it was that was holding them back; they were lighter and looked and held themselves differently, and carried a completely different energy with them. I was seeing true transformations, complete transformations, unfolding before my eyes.

Of course, it's not a miracle cure. Some of it worked quickly for a lot of people, but for others it took a bit longer, yet it worked, over and over again. My clients started coming back and they were reporting changes within themselves, their relationships, with their communication, their health and their overall wellbeing.

I've never really been one to accept things as finite. I've always liked to explore them further and come up with exciting and innovative approaches to things, especially if I've been told it 'won't work'. I like to think outside the square and I guess, if I'm totally honest, I've been a bit of a square peg in a round hole for much of my life in many ways. So when I was told that a certain approach was the 'gold standard' in treatment, I learnt it and turned myself inside out mastering it, but I never accepted that it was the only way. I kept wondering how I could make it even better, or perhaps if there were other options or ways to look at it, and that has been what has led to the development of my treatment model.

When I'd completed hundreds of client sessions around the process of letting go of the trauma or the issue that was keeping them stuck, and actually moving forward, I realised that I needed to put it together with some other strategies that enabled it to come together as a whole system, an entire treatment process. With a combination of a number of theories and foundational models, I have developed what I now refer to as my ABS system, or Accelerated Breakthrough Strategies system that effectively treats trauma or issues that are keeping you stuck, and assists you to release these issues and find true freedom.

There are a number of areas that I have brought together in developing this approach. My ABS Model utilises a combination of some self-discrepancy theory, developed by Edward Tory Higgins, where we look at the three components of self: actual, ideal and ought self. I'll go into more detail about those in future chapters.

This is combined with some foundational concepts that look at the components of identity, values and some core beliefs, which we all have either consciously or unconsciously. I've utilised this with some components of Matrix Therapy, developed by Pip McKay, and some Deep State Re-Patterning (DSR), developed by Alice Haemmerle and Sharon Pearson who have extended upon the work of Richard Bandler and John Grinder (NLP founders) and Tony Robbins and Tad James. This is combined with some work from the drug and alcohol field by Dr Michael Crowley around Empowerment Therapy.

There's also some information at the core underlying the ABS Model from the field of M-Braining, which is the work of Marvin Oka and Grant Soosalu, based on the latest neuroscience insights. It uses NLP and behavioural modelling with some work around the three brains (the brain in our head, our heart and our gut), as well as a lot of research from the field of neuroscience around neuroplasticity and the ability we have to change our brains, which was particularly noted in the book by Norman Doidge, *The Brain that Changes Itself*.

So, as I've said, after years of gathering information, years of training, I've managed to put everything that I know together into an effective, succinct and efficient therapy known as ABS therapy.

Clients no longer needed to come in for long-term therapy, for years and years of working through their trauma or the issue that was keeping them stuck somewhere they weren't happy with, getting frustrated that the counselling was giving them neither the outcome that they wanted nor getting them there as quickly as what they felt they wanted it to be.

Not only was their frustration evident, but mine became evident as well, before putting together the ABS model, at seeing the pain in these people's faces and their mannerisms when I couldn't give them the 'magic pill' and breakthrough that they wanted.

But with the ABS model, I was blown away at the results I was getting. One of the clients who stands out in particular was Stacey. Stacey was a lady in her forties who had been through significant trauma and had carried it around with her for seven years. It had impacted every part of her life: her relationship had broken down, she was a single mother, with one eight-year-old daughter who she didn't feel overly connected to. She felt as though she was exhausted, she was always angry, she just didn't have the relationships in her life that she wanted, she kept to herself, she worked in a job she hated and she felt really disengaged and disconnected from the world around her.

When speaking with her in the initial session, she showed very little emotion the majority of the time. However, when we looked at what was really going on with her current functioning, she burst into tears saying she couldn't stand it any more. After two sessions using the ABS model, she was booked in for her third session and was sitting in the waiting room when my receptionist knocked on my door and said, 'Your next client's here, I don't know who she is. She looks like someone else, she looks a bit like Stacey. It's supposed to be Stacey that you've seen before, but she looks nothing like her!'

It turned out that the change was so significant the time before, after the second session, that Stacey had been impacted completely. She looked different, she had even worn make-up to the session, she dressed differently, she held herself differently, it was like the weight of the world had been lifted off her shoulders. She reported that she'd had a great week with her daughter, that she'd resigned from her job, applied for a new job and she'd gotten an interview for it. She had slept well, her skin looked clearer, she had more energy and confidence. The change in her was nothing short of unbelieveable, and what I was seeing was that changes like this were happening on a regular basis across multiple clients, regardless of their presenting issues.

I kept working with hundreds of clients and the results continued in a consistent manner. Some of my colleagues started asking me what I was doing and how I was getting the results I was getting; they started to ask some more questions and I would tell them what I was doing.

Unfortunately, what I found was that many therapists were closed to new ways of doing things. They were stuck in old patterns of training. Don't get me wrong, I'm not saying that there is anything bad or incorrect about the therapies or approaches that they use. They do work and are effective, but mostly they are slower than what I wanted for my clients.

While this might be going against the norm, I felt that my results spoke for themselves. It's a bit like the picture that did the rounds on Facebook ages ago of the overweight man in the mankini. It certainly wasn't a pretty sight; it was one of those things that once seen, it could not be unseen. I liken that to this: once I knew of this way of treatment, I couldn't 'un-know' it. In fact, I felt I was doing a disservice to my clients, the people whose lives I wanted to change, not to teach this process. I felt it would be irresponsible not to continue to work with the people I was working with, given the results they were getting and the significant changes overall.

Imagine the big picture, imagine the changes in an individual, if we're all able to find a way of working through things and letting go efficiently and the ripple effects of not holding onto trauma or negative emotions that hold us back and keep us stuck. Imagine the ripple effects on a family, on a community. Imagine if other professionals could be trained in this method and they could utilise it to have a flow on effect with their clients. We could really make huge ripples in the world.

We all know that *one* person who we walk on eggshells around because of the impact of upsetting them and the impact of such on everyone else in their world. If we can make a difference in the life of just one person, it has a flow-on effect to all in their lives.

We used to believe not so long ago that the brain cells we were born with were what we had for the rest of our lives and they gradually died off. But what we now know through years of neuroscience research is that the brain has plasticity. Neuroplasticity exists and it is real.

So I invite you to join me now on my journey as I move from working one-on-one with clients to working one-to-many, educating other professionals and starting conversations about the ABS model, working on changing lives by getting to the source of the issue through my book and offering an introduction to the ABS model that will undoubtedly facilitate significant change and offering further trainings with a ripple effect to change the lives of many rather than one person at a time.

Chapter 3
Transformational Model (Seven Steps)

"Your calling isn't something that somebody can tell you about. It's what you feel. It is the thing that gives you juice. The thing that you are supposed to do. And nobody can tell you what that is. You know it inside yourself."

Oprah Winfrey

Now it's time to reveal this seven-step model. These seven steps are what I truly believe will take you from trauma to triumph, frustration to freedom.

The ABS system is a seven-step system, taking you through all the areas that you need to go in order to experience true transformation. It's been tried and tested on hundreds and hundreds of my clients, regardless of their presenting issues, their types of trauma, their types of issues and challenges, and all of them have come out with amazing outcomes and complete transformations.

As I've already mentioned, I didn't just put a few things together, try it once and that was it. It was trialled, tested and measured, and there was certainly error along the way. But I honestly believe, and the clients I've worked with have given me very clear feedback, that their lives have changed and they've changed, deep at the core, forever, not just for the short term. They feel that they can see a future for themselves now, one that will fulfil their dreams of being exactly who they have always wanted to be.

So if you no longer want to talk and talk and talk and have to engage in never-ending therapy for years on end, you're frustrated, you're at the end of your tether and you want a solution quickly, like yesterday, I encourage you to keep reading and embark on understanding and then implementing the entire seven-step process.

It's really important that the seven steps are followed in order to ensure that it flows and things don't remain stuck.

Please don't be put off; it doesn't necessarily mean seven separate sessions, as over and over again I've found that we can get results one on one in as few as three sessions – life-changing results – but we always work through the seven clear steps of the model.

I cannot reiterate enough that it's important we follow all seven steps, so that you fully understand the process, what you need to work through and how to redefine yourself fully to create the future, that you've dreamt of and that you desire.

This seven-step model, the ABS system, is a comprehensive model that addresses all the components that I know from years of experience need to surface and be fully addressed in order to experience a true transformation.

Let me tell you about one of the wonderful people I worked with. He was a police officer named Darren. Darren had experienced years of traumas, multiple traumas, things that human beings just should never be exposed to.

He presented as suicidal, his family relationships had broken down, he was a father of two young children with whom he had barely any relationship due to his anger, his frustrations, and his complete disconnection from family relationships as he felt he 'wasn't deserving of being loved'.

Darren came to me at a time when I hadn't done all the training that I have now done and we 'stabilised' him. He was no longer suicidal; however, he decided he could not be a police officer on an ongoing basis anymore and we worked on getting him out of the career that he loved. It was who he believed he was, it had become his entire identity, it was all he knew.

I put him through my ABS system which I had developed by then. He presented with such complex trauma that he did need some more sessions than what many of my clients have needed.

However, within the seven-step sessions, he had been able to process a lot of the things that were causing him significant distress, his relationship improved with his wife, he had reconnected with his children, he had started investing in a hobby that he loved that went on to become a viable business for him.

He reported improved sleep with no further nightmares, he'd ceased drinking to excess and he felt that he was actually living his life again.

Yes, he had to grieve the loss of the identity as he knew it and create a new identity, new values, new beliefs and new behaviours but when I saw him recently to catch up, he looked like a new person. He was almost vibrant and he was calm.

The ABS Model

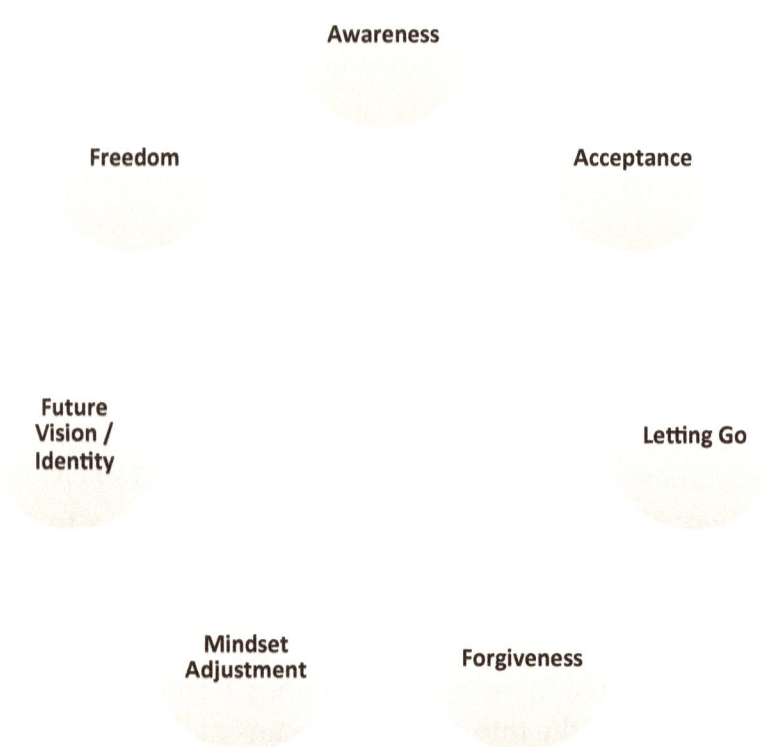

1 Awareness
Gain an understanding of who you are as a person, as an individual, understand your behaviours, what drives your behaviour, what values underlie this and what belief system you hold for yourself. You need to be very clear on your identity, who you are, who you believe yourself to be, incorporating the many roles you play in your life.

2 Acceptance
Accept yourself for who you are right now and understand that your current behaviours are not serving you effectively at this moment in time, we start preparing you to move your actual self towards the ideal self that you hold in your mind.

3 Letting Go

We need to understand the need to let go of things, the importance of no longer holding on to emotional baggage and hurts, to negative beliefs, values and behaviours that are self-destructive and destructive to those around us that we love. It's about moving towards what we want rather than continuing to move away from the pain, reinforcing patterns where we keep getting more of the pain. It's about letting go of the feelings that will come up for us as we engage in this process, it's about finding the courage to acknowledge what we're experiencing and being prepared to be vulnerable and let go of this emotion to create the life that we choose for ourselves.

4 Forgiveness

This is often a very challenging concept, understanding the need to forgive. The true meaning of forgiveness is not about erasing it from your memory but simply choosing to forgive in order to free yourself from the bitterness that holding on to this baggage continues to bring you. The memory stays, not to be forgotten, but to be remembered as a valuable lesson for you. It's about understanding not only the need to forgive, but the power of forgiveness, in its true meaning. It is important to forgive others, not necessarily because they deserve forgiveness, but because you deserve peace. It's about going full circle, being able to forgive ourselves, which is the absolute ultimate in getting on with our lives.

5 Mindset Adjustment

Learn to think again, understand your values, redefine them, as well as your beliefs. Start to establish your new identity, how you want to be, who you want to be and understand fully that being vulnerable is okay. When we have the courage to really feel our emotions and be raw and vulnerable, we also have the capacity to heal.

6 Future Vision and Identity
Design the future that you want for yourself, have the people that you want in your life and develop hope to live a life that is meaningful and fulfilling, just as you deserve.

7 Freedom
Understanding the old world that you've left behind versus the new world. Step fully into the new world that you are creating, the new you and your ability to shape your own future, your ability to love your actual self and move it to be more aligned with your ideal self. Have the courage to be vulnerable and enable yourself to thrive.

As I have said this model has been developed for use through working with hundreds and hundreds of clients in my private practice – clients presenting with a wide range of issues, from anger, anxiety, depression, grief and loss, to significant trauma – and it has been proven to be effective across all of these areas.

Of course, as you're reading this book, you could choose not to do this process, not to see the value in it. What's the worst thing that could happen? You could stay the same, that nothing could change. You might choose not to engage in the process as it's far easier to stay comfortable. That old saying, it's 'better the devil you know'…

However, will you always be wondering, 'what if? What if I did do this? What if my life were different?'

You could choose to stay stuck, to stay and play small, to keep things exactly as they are. You can live a life half-lived.

OR you could choose to give it a go, to follow the process and complete all seven steps of the ABS system in order, because you and the important people in your life are worth it.

Chapter 3 – Transformational Model (Seven Steps)

So as you move forward on this journey with me, from now until the end of the book, we will complete some practical exercises at the end of each chapter. This will take you through the process itself and help you to take action. We know that results only come through action and implementation.

To make it somewhat easier for you, I have included a bonus *free* downloadable workbook on my website that accompanies this book. Please go to **www.drnataliegreen.com.au/ABSWorkbook** and register your details to get direct access to the downloadable workbook.

Action

As a result of reading this chapter, I ask you to take out a piece of paper, or use the downloadable workbook provided, or draw it on a whiteboard, whatever works best for you. I want you to do what we term a 'cost-benefit analysis'.

You can draw a cross on the page or whiteboard so you now have four quadrants. In the top two quadrants I want you to write 'costs' on the left-hand side and 'benefits' on the right-hand side. In the bottom two quadrants I want you to write 'costs' and 'benefits' again. The top half is for you to write down the costs and the benefits to you and the people that are important in your life if you choose not to utilise the ABS system; down the bottom, write the costs and the benefits if you choose to follow the ABS system. I want you to be honest; no one else needs to see it. Just write down absolutely everything.

- What will it cost you if nothing changes?
- What are the benefits to you if nothing changes?

That might sound really strange, but really we know that when people identify the need to change their behaviour but choose not to, it's usually because there's something in it for them not to. That might be fear of what happens if it doesn't work; that might be fear of feeling too uncomfortable or fear of 'what if the people I love don't like me any more?' There can be all sorts of things.

Down the bottom again you'll need to be really honest with yourself.

- What are the costs of doing the ABS system?
- What are the benefits to you for doing it?

And then it should be very clear to you which choice you are going to make. Will you follow the ABS system or will you leave things as they are? It's totally up to you.

Chapter 4
Trauma Unlocked

"Although the world is full of suffering, it is full also of the overcoming of it."
Helen Keller

When we think of trauma, there are so many things that come to mind. There are multiple forms of trauma. You might find yourself, as you read this book, minimising the things that have happened to you, thinking, 'Oh, that's not that traumatic' or 'that's not really determined as a trauma' or 'I should be able to just get on with things'.

But I challenge you right now to stop that way of thinking and recognise that if you have negative feelings or negative emotions that feel as though they are stuck somewhere within your mind, within your heart or within your gut, if you get a feeling in any one of those three areas (what they now determine as having neurons and therefore being brains), I would suggest to you that this book *is* for you.

It could well be that you have a type of trauma that you could benefit from identifying, acknowledging, accepting and letting go of so that you can have the life that you deserve and that you choose to create.

As I have mentioned previously, being traumatised does *not* mean you had to witness someone die or see or experience something so horrific that you could never repeat it to anyone. No. There are so many things that I believe constitute trauma and some that might simply be distressing enough to you that you feel you simply can't 'shake'.

Psychological distress following exposure to a traumatic or stressful event is quite variable. There is no right or wrong; if you have experienced a considerable reaction, then it may constitute a trauma for you.

Remember, trauma won't just show itself as anxiety and fear, but instead it can also present itself as an inability to feel anything much at all, or a general dissatisfaction with life right through to anger and aggressive behaviours.

The word 'trauma' is derived from the Greek term for 'wound'. Very frightening or distressing events may result in a psychological wound or injury – especially a difficulty in coping or functioning normally following a particular event or experience. Everyone's reaction is different, and most people who experience a potentially traumatic event will recover well with the help of family and friends and will not experience any long-term problems. If people do develop problems, they may appear directly after the traumatic event or they may not emerge until much later.

Let's not forget that everyone has their own filtering system that applies to every experience they have in the world and, as we've already covered, the same event may have little impact on one person but cause severe distress in another individual. There is no right or wrong, it simply is what it is. The impact that an event has may be related to the person's mental and physical health, level of available support at the time of the event, and past experience and coping skills.

Let me highlight for you what can constitute a trauma and you may realise that you too really have experienced one and could benefit from allowing yourself to acknowledge it and process it fully.

The stock standard way of thinking about trauma is when you've witnessed someone dying, or you've been in a car accident, or that you've been the victim of assault, or sexual, physical or emotional abuse, or you've been involved in a serious incident.

However, if you've experienced a natural disaster, whether it be a flood, an earthquake, a fire or a major storm that's caused damage; a motor vehicle or workplace accident; a form of grief and loss, the injury or illness or death of a loved one, your own long-term chronic illness; domestic violence, a relationship breakdown, bullying, neglect, abandonment, a threat of harm to yourself or to others; if you're an emergency services worker who's been to multiple incidents or you've been to just one of them – that is all a form of trauma and a wound that you need to heal.

Let me now run through various types of trauma.

Acute trauma
Exposure to a single overwhelming event or experience, like a motor vehicle accident, a natural disaster, a one-off assault or abuse, a sudden loss of someone you love or something that you love, witnessing violence, the loss of someone through suicide – these are all incidents of acute trauma.

Repetitive trauma
Exposure to multiple chronic and/or prolonged overwhelming traumatic events, such as receiving regular treatment for a serious illness or a sexual assault that is repeated, or domestic violence.

Complex trauma
It results from multiple chronic and prolonged or overwhelming events or experiences, most often within a context of an interpersonal relationship such as domestic violence, or emotional abuse, or sexual abuse. Emergency services workers also experience complex trauma, often on a long-term basis from the ongoing impact of their years of service.

Developmental trauma
It results from early onset exposure to ongoing or repetitive trauma as an infant, child or adolescent. It can include neglect, abandonment, emotional, physical or sexual abuse or assault, witnessing violence or a death, coercion or betrayal. It often occurs within the child's care-giving system and it interferes with healthy attachment and development.

Vicarious trauma
This occurs when an individual who was not an immediate witness to the trauma itself absorbs and integrates disturbing aspects of the traumatic experience into their own functioning. This is often seen within service providers such as counsellors, psychologists, clergy workers. It results from empathetic engagement with the client's trauma background.

As I have said earlier, I have worked in the trauma field for over twenty-five years and unfortunately there honestly is not much I haven't seen or heard by now.

One of the greatest unspoken things in our industry for many of those years was the impact that hearing about the trauma had on us as professionals. We were meant to just 'suck it up' and hear the stories days in and day out and brush it off. If we were lucky, we had supervision and could debrief about things and the impact they had on us.

However, many of us tended to just get on with things for fear of being seen as weak. I, for one, certainly didn't feel that I could expose my vulnerability in case people thought I was no longer able to do my job.

There was ego involved and a hell of a lot of pride, but it certainly came at a cost, I know that now.

Let me tell you a story that is very close to my heart and demonstrates how trauma and hearing about people's stories can impact on you and how it might show itself in ways that don't necessarily mean suffering severe anxiety or fear responses.

As I briefly mentioned earlier in the beginning of the book, I worked at Port Arthur after the massacre that occurred there in 1996. I don't tend to talk about it much, but it had a profound impact on me as a person, and was a huge turning point for me in many ways. I worked at Port Arthur for one year with the employees of the site and also with many of the people who were there on the day who suffered untold trauma as part of what they experienced and witnessed.

I worked ridiculously long hours, generally doing sixteen-hour days and working seven days per week for the majority of that year. I threw myself into my work, desperate to do the best job possible in a very challenging situation. I kept myself as busy as I could and tried to be all things to all people. I did manage to build a small network of support people with some other allied health professionals who worked in varying capacities in the nearby communities.

We used to speak a bit, we spent short bursts of time together and occasionally had dinner together; however, we really never spoke about what we saw or heard. We simply got on with it as we felt that was what was required of us.

I didn't feel depressed, I didn't notice major anxiety (except on one occasion where I heard some strange and loud noises on the roof of my shack one night, which turned out to be a rogue possum – lol). Looking back now, I do recall one specific event part way through my time there that really should have been an indicator that I probably should have asked for help along the way.

It was during the time of the offender's trial. Prior to its commencement, many of the people who had been at Port Arthur on the day were brought back down to the actual site of the traumatic event. It was a well coordinated visit with considerable support services available to anyone who wished to attend. Of significant note was that the area was deemed a 'no-fly' zone, due to the significant trauma attached to the sound of the helicopters from the day and also due to privacy reasons.

I clearly remember that we were walking through the old café with some of the people who bravely chose to return there and we were dealing with the significant trauma responses that this brought with it. This was an extremely emotional time and the distress involved in that day is still very clear to me now.

All of a sudden I realised that the no-fly zone restriction had been breached and there were high profile media people there. Of note was one particular very high profile reporter, who had arrived by helicopter close by, and who was sitting in a van with the cameras aimed directly on the highly distressed and traumatised people who were being taken through the café area.

That was it. I saw red. I ensured that the people we were with were moved back into a safe area and being taken care of before I stormed down to the van that was sitting on the open area. I absolutely lost it verbally, telling the reporter

Chapter 4 – Trauma Unlocked

to 'shove his camera up his f***ing a*se'. Thankfully, the cameras and men actually went back into the van; they sat there for a long time, no longer recording what was happening. I was absolutely livid.

Certainly not my proudest moment; however, at the time I felt it was my job to protect these people from the intrusiveness and additional distress this would bring upon them. I wanted to minimise the significant distress for these people as much as possible. In the big picture, what I did probably didn't make much difference, but it was important to me. That was a clear indicator that I had been impacted by the significance of the work I was doing but just hadn't admitted it to myself (or anyone else). Interestingly, I still cannot watch that reporter on television or in any capacity as it brings things flooding back over twenty years later (and it's now a clear choice that I make on principle, rather than because I'm still traumatised by it).

I did eventually speak up and sought help once I returned home after I had completed my work down there. I was approved for 'one session' and after attending that I was able to normalise my response and what I was feeling, processing it all in a healthy way and gradually moving on and continuing to do my job in as productive a way as possible.

However, no one is immune to trauma and the impact it can have. I kept telling myself the massacre hadn't happened to me, I didn't have the right to have a reaction like I did and that I just needed to put it behind me and get on with it. However, that strategy didn't really serve me and I carried the impact of the trauma around with me for many years to come until I eventually allowed myself to experience my ABS system. I made the decision to embrace my vulnerability, feel the emotion attached to that period of my life and give myself permission to process it fully and completely so I could actively move forward. While I engaged in some self-care and attempted to uphold my boundaries, this experience undoubtedly changed me at the core. I couldn't 'un-see', 'un-hear' or 'un-experience' the things that I did and I had to learn a way to process this and put it away so it didn't change me forever.

Through utilising my ABS system on myself, I have now been able to process all of that, compartmentalise it and put it inside the box within a section of my brain and close the lid. I can access that at any time or I can choose to keep the lid on. It's totally up to me and I'm okay with that.

So I write this to let you know that no one is immune to trauma and distressing events, information and experiences and to encourage you not to minimise your experience of trauma or distress. Acknowledge that if you are demonstrating anxiety, fear, anhedonia, dysphoria, agitation or anger, ask yourself where it has really come from and what could really be going on. Actively seek help or apply the ABS model so you can let the negative emotions go and live the life you want again.

Historical inter-generational trauma

This is a psychological trauma that can affect cultural groups, communities and/or generations. It can be around racism, colonisation, loss of culture, removal from family, community, genocide or war. What we have seen is that coping and adaptation patterns have developed in response to trauma and can then be passed on through generations.

A case study that comes to mind is a wonderful client that I had some years ago, an Aboriginal lady in her late forties; let's call her Jane. She had been removed from her family at a young age and placed in an institution out in the outback, run by well respected Aboriginal community members.

Chapter 4 – Trauma Unlocked

Not only was she subjected to removal from her family and the attachment to her primary caregiver interrupted at a critical age, she also experienced significant ongoing complex trauma by way of child sexual assault over many years by someone she was supposed to trust. This occurred along with significant exposure to drug and alcohol and abuse and significant physical and emotional violence. When she presented for treatment as an adult, her life was, as she described, 'extremely dysfunctional'.

She barely left her house, she drank herself to oblivion, she used drugs. She had children who had also been removed and she felt significant guilt and shame around this. We engaged her in the ABS system. We took her through the entire process. She was able to not only report her abuse to the police but was able to go to court, speak up for herself and lead many other females to speak up about what had happened to them; a successful class action has been completed.

She has been able to re-establish an excellent relationship with her children who are now adults. She has ceased drinking, she has engaged in volunteer work in her community, she's been able to establish sound, healthy relationships with some friends and is now in a healthy, non-violent relationship with her partner. Most of all, she feels that she is living again, she knows who she is, she knows what she stands for and she has established some clear boundaries and ongoing self-care. Her self-worth is much improved and she feels she has transformed her life.

If you've gotten to this point and you're still minimising what you've been through, or maybe have started thinking, 'well, maybe it was traumatic', I would suggest that you complete the life stress questionnaire in *Appendix* 2 to determine how many of these things you have also experienced. They may not be the specific traumas I've referred to above, but are certainly situations that can evoke significant stress and cause a 'wound' in the person you are. Be aware of what your score is and whether maybe, just maybe, you have some significant stress or negative emotion that is stuck within you that is impacting your relationships, your life, your health or some area of your life and whether it might be time for you to engage in the ABS process and take yourself through from your trauma to triumph and ultimately to freedom.

Chapter 5

The Awakening

"Life's challenges are not supposed to paralyse you; they're supposed to help you discover who you are."
Bernice Johnson Reagon

No doubt you've spent most of your life being aware of who you are, what you like, what you don't like, what's important to you, and why you behave in the way that you do. You've always been pretty clear in knowing your values and your beliefs, how you'll react when any of this is compromised or challenged.

To embark on fully embracing the ABS model, it's essential that you have an awareness, an understanding of your behaviours, your values, your identity, who you are at this point in your life *now*, as it is highly likely that this may be different to how you used to be as a result of what you have experienced.

If you're reading this, most likely you've been through something, maybe even lots of things. It may even have been that the person that you knew, and who you were happy with, was lost years ago and you're only just coming to terms with this now, knowing that things are different for you now. You feel sad, maybe even really depressed, disillusioned with things and how they're turning out. You might be quite agitated or reactive whereas you used to be easy-going and a 'go with the flow' type of person. You worry a lot now, about even the slightest things, or about what other people think.

You've become short-tempered, frustrated, angry and snipey at things and the people you care the most about. Or you've gone to the other extreme and you don't worry about anything. You don't care at all when you know you should.

You've stopped doing the things that you used to do, that you really enjoyed, most likely you've disconnected from friends, from family members and at times it's like you're in your own little world. If you're honest, that's actually how you like it. You can't remember the last time you've slept properly; you toss and turn all night. If you get to sleep, you might have flashbacks, nightmares or night sweats and you wake up exhausted and have to do it all over again.

It's all taking a toll on your health. You've got a sense of fatigue, of tightness in your head. You have headaches, blood pressure issues, blood sugar issues. You may have put on weight as you comfort yourself with food or you may be protecting yourself so no one notices you anymore. Or you may have gone to the other extreme and you've lost weight as your appetite is non-existent, or perhaps you've turned to alcohol, cigarettes or even drugs to manage your pain.

You have low energy, aches and pains, random complaints that your doctor either dismisses or doesn't even know the answer for. You've even questioned whether it's all in your head.

The biggest thing, though, is that you are recognising that these things are not you, they're not your version of normal and you certainly don't want to accept these behaviours and ways of being as your status quo.

Let's now explore the concept of self that comes from the work of E. Tory Higgins. Within each of us lies the concept that there are three components of self that we all have. There is the Ideal Self, the Actual Self and the Ought Self.

Ideal Self
You hold in your mind a version of yourself that you strive for, an image and a feeling of exactly how you want things to be for you and how you want to experience things in your own little world. It is a version of you with aspirations, with goals, with a vision of how you want to be and how you want your life to be.

Actual Self
This is based on how you actually are, what your functional level is right now and what you're capable of being and doing right now at this point in your life, both physically and emotionally.

Ought Self
This is the part of ourselves that is based on the expectations we believe others have for us. It is how we think we ought to be and behave, and what we perceive we should be able to do. It is where all the 'shoulds' are held: 'you should do this', 'you should be like this', 'you should be able to do this'.

When any of the three selves are out of alignment, in particular our Actual Self with either the Ideal or Ought Self, we can run into difficulties with coping overall. These differences are what is known as 'Self Discrepancy'; this is where conflicts arise for you.

It is within the Self Discrepancy area that you are likely living right now as a result of what has happened in your life and whatever pain you are carrying around with you right now.

When your Actual Self is so far removed from what you want to feel like (your Ideal Self), you feel like giving in and running away; you just have no idea what to do next. Your Ideal Self versus your Actual Self are like two completely different people and you recognise the self-hatred that has been creeping in for quite a while now.

Then there's the expectation that others have for you or that you think others hold for you. 'You should be doing this', 'you should be feeling like this', 'thinking this', etc. This Ought Self versus your Actual Self are poles apart as you simply don't have the energy to live up to anyone's expectations right now.

So for a long time you've likely worn a mask. You've put it on and hidden what is going on within you from the world. You have become so good at it that at times you may even convince yourself that this masquerade is your new reality. You wear your mask so well, you have become accustomed to the pressure it places on your face, the view from behind it, cutting off your peripheral vision to a degree. You see a different and somewhat distorted view and no one really knows any different – or so you think!

In order to move forward, it is now time to create the awakening you need to head towards the freedom that you desire.

While this may feel somewhat confronting as you start to think through this, it is important to understand who you are versus who you used to be, so you can recognise the changes that have occurred, that have taken place within you so you can start to move forward.

Being really clear on who you always thought you were and your ideal sense of you, who you expect yourself to be, indeed your Ideal Self, is very important to understand, as is the need to be very clear on who you actually are now: Your Actual Self with your values, your beliefs, and your identity based on your current reality. It is essential that you understand the Ideal versus the Actual Self right now.

Actual Self
- Who am I now?
- What role can I do now?
- What am I able to do right now?
- What is important to me right now?
- What do I believe is possible right now?

Ideal Self
- Who do I want to be?
- What roles do I want to do?
- What do I want to be able to do?
- What do I want to be important to me?
- What would I like to believe is possible for me?

Ought Self
- Who do others think I should be?
- What roles do others think I should do?
- What do others say/think I should be able to do?
- What do others think should be important to me?
- What do others believe is possible for me?

Action

Exercise 2: old me versus new me

Now take out a piece of paper or open the workbook that you have downloaded from **www.drnataliegreen.com.au/ABSWorkbook**. On the left-hand side I want you to put 'old me' with a line down the centre and then on the right-hand side, 'new me'. Under 'old me' write 'Ideal Self' and in that column write a list of what you wanted to be, the dreams, the aspirations you had for yourself, your values, your beliefs, your identity, all those things, so you are really clear on that old version of you. On the right-hand side, write a list of the Actual Self, the feelings, the emotions, the values, the beliefs that you also hold, right now in your current reality.

Know that at this point in time it is perfectly okay for there to be a significant difference between your Ideal Self and your Actual Self. This is your Self Discrepancy.

I want you to be honest and ask yourself, what is it truly costing you to hide behind that mask? What is the impact of pretending everything is okay, is 'picture perfect' in your world? What is the real impact on you of doing this?

How are your relationships really? Are they equal, is there open and honest communication and appropriate two-way give and take?

How is your emotional health? If you are absolutely honest with yourself, are you calm and feeling at peace within yourself? Or are you on edge, constantly worrying about others and what others think, and never thinking about you and what's going on within you?

How is your physical health? Are you at your ideal weight, are you feeling fit and healthy, are you feeling energetic and on top of things? Or is your reality telling a completely different story behind that mask you wear?

Chapter 5 – The Awakening

Are you ready to be honest, to tell the truth and acknowledge your own reality as it is right now?

Let's face it, there are many things you simply cannot change, that you have no control over whatsoever. So it is about accepting your reality, reflecting on it and making the adjustments you need. Embracing your vulnerability is essential for you to get the changes and the success in your life that you desire.

Action
Exercise 3: the circle of impact

The step I'd like you to take next is to make a list of the impact that you honestly believe the trauma/distress that you have gone through this has had on your life. It's essential that you have clarity around the whole effect that it's had on your life, not to compartmentalise it so it feels like it's only had a small impact, or has impacted only small bits of your life.

Yes, it will feel uncomfortable, but in order for us to move forward and process this and let go of it completely, we must have awareness. This is necessary before we can change any part of our lives and ourselves.

In the workbook, draw a circle in the middle of the page with your name in it. Then draw multiple lines from the centre outwards with all the areas of your life that you believe have been impacted as a result of what has happened in your life and how you have reacted to it. Be completely honest. Include such things as your relationships, your family life, your self-esteem, your self-belief, your identity as a whole, your work capacity, your friendships etc. Include *every* area of your life you believe has been affected by this issue.

As you start to see the reality of the changes this trauma has had on your life, undoubtedly the discomfort may rise and the pain may surface. But know that this is temporary as we are about to engage in the next component, which is moving us away from what we no longer want to be part of our lives and towards how we want our lives to be.

It is important to *acknowledge* your situation, have awareness around your current reality and *accept* it for what it is right now. This does not mean that it will stay this way forever, yet right now it is what it is and then you can make some *adjustments*.

The simplest way to make those adjustments is to be really clear on what and who you used to be (i.e. your Ideal Self, the vision you had for yourself as you were) and have absolute clarity around your Actual Self and what you are actually capable of right now in the present moment, ensuring you take into account your physical, psychological and your emotional health and all the things that you have no control over (i.e. the curve balls that have come your way). Adjust your perceptions and expectations of your Actual Self to be more in alignment and for your Ideal Self to be as close as possible to your Actual Self for now.

This does not mean you are accepting less than you want for yourself, that you are lowering your standards or are a failure; the reality is so far from that. By adjusting your expectations of self and bringing them together in the short term, you are dissolving the internal conflicts that have arisen and you are making the changes necessary to drop your pretence, to lower your mask and let people experience you as you are – genuine, honest and raw and vulnerable, the person they have likely always wanted you to be.

In order to move forward, bringing that into our awareness, and knowing that there is a difference between the old you and the current you, means that you can see very clearly that there is room to move and that there are things to let go of, so you can become ready to start the process. Don't spend too much time on this, don't judge yourself. Just write it down, know your reality and own it. Become aware of it and experience a true awakening.

Chapter 6
Finding Courage

"I learned that courage was not the absence of fear, but the triumph over it. The brave man is not he who does not feel afraid, but he who conquers that fear."

Nelson Mandela

Knowing and understanding that who you have become right now (i.e. your Actual Self) is not aligned with who you want to be and where you want to stay long-term is more than half the battle won.

Having awareness around your situation and seeing the discrepancies between your current reality and how things used to be and how you would like them to be provides the motivation that we need to move us through from the awakening stage into acceptance.

Accepting that your current reality is not what you want to live for yourself longer term, that the pain of what you are feeling right now far outweighs the pleasure that you gain from being stuck, forms the motivation that you need to help project yourself forward.

Let me introduce the concept of 'moving away versus moving towards'. Think of this concept as being two different ends of one spectrum. On the left-hand side, you have the concept of moving away from pain and on the right-hand side, the other end of the spectrum, is someone who's driven by moving towards pleasure. It's a pain-versus-pleasure concept. People who are motivated or driven by moving away from something generally want to avoid a certain situation. They don't want to experience loss or discomfort; they want to move away from something, from pain, and are motivated by avoiding the pain they are experiencing. 'Moving away from' people will tell you what they don't want. They will talk about what they don't like, what they can't do, the threats they perceive, the avoidance of pain and they often complain.

When you look back at the language you use, if you say, 'I don't want this any more', 'I can't stand that', 'I don't like this', you are most likely motivated by moving away from something.

This quote by Aristotle sums this up quite well for someone with a 'moving away from' motivation: 'The aim of the wise is not to secure pleasure but to avoid pain'.

When one has a 'moving away' perspective, we notice there is a desire to avoid things, rather than focus on what one can achieve. When they move far enough away from the pain, they give themselves permission to stay where they are, once they get to where they feel comfortable again.

What we can see, however, is that when someone is motivated by moving away from pain and they get to a place where they are feeling comfortable, they can often self-sabotage so they get back to experiencing more pain, so as they can move away from that again, as that is what they know and where they feel most comfortable.

People who are motivated by moving towards something

always strive to achieve an outcome. They want to and focus on what they will get when the outcome is achieved. They are moving towards pleasure, motivated by gaining pleasure. 'Moving towards' people will tell you what they want. They will talk about what they like, what they can do, the possibilities they perceive, the attraction to goals and will often focus on solutions.

So with your language right now, if it tends to be, 'I want this', 'I want to be positive and empowering', you are already well on your way to being 'moving towards' motivated.

As we work through this concept, it's really important that you understand that one is not right and one is not wrong, that it's only natural when you've experienced trauma or are feeling the impact of past traumas and the pain associated with this, that your preferred motivation is generally around moving away from the pain due to the negativity associated with this and the huge negative energy you perceive it would take to focus on the moving towards process.

What I love about this ABS system is that utilising the entire seven-step process transitions you from primarily moving away to primarily moving towards. At its conclusion you recognise that when you focus on possibilities and solutions, you can create your future as you decide you want it to be for you.

The ABS model allows you to let go of fears that you have worked hard to avoid, and replace these with positive, self-affirming, empowering goals that serve your life purpose and move you towards where you want to head, rather than feeling as though you're constantly being driven by negative energy and pressure by moving away from something.

Accepting that you have these things going on in your life and within you, by truly understanding them, you can acknowledge the "not-so-great" parts that have infiltrated into your existence and your identity right now. Then you are truly ready to seek and become courageous.

The true meaning of courage is 'the ability to do something that frightens you'. Today having courage is synonymous with being heroic (and we certainly need heroes), but having true courage, I feel is more about speaking honestly and openly about who you are, about what you are feeling and about your experiences, both good and bad, and truly owning them.

I believe that the work of Brené Brown (*Daring Greatly*, 2015) was phenomenal and life-changing in many ways. She researched, then lived her findings. Her work focuses on having the courage to be vulnerable, to really feel the pain, the negative emotions and negative feelings, and to sit with those emotions and feelings in order to move forward.

I too have done the same in my own life transformations. I've learnt that in order to move beyond my own trauma and my own experiences into true freedom, we must first find the courage to be vulnerable. It is about acknowledging the gap between our Ideal and our Actual Self and the fact that we are most likely driven by moving away from the pain rather than moving towards the outcome and the desire that we want.

In order for you to embrace your vulnerability right now and step into the power, you have to experience true courage, then be clear on your biggest driver or motivator right now. Are you motivated mainly to move away or move towards at this point in time?

Take note of the language you tend to use in your conversations on a daily basis with people and identify where you sit on that continuum. Are you in the middle, are you more on the left side or towards the right side? Put a mark on there as to where you are right now.

Make a list of anything that you feel within your body if you sat right now with your eyes closed and did a complete 'scan' of your body: from the tip of your head, right through your neck, your shoulders, your chest, your stomach, your abdomen, right down your pelvis, down your legs, right through to the tip of your toes. Get in touch with every part of your body where you feel any niggly discomfort or perhaps even physical pain. Have the courage to sit with that. Don't do anything with it right now; just make a note of where you feel that. Just allow yourself to feel it and sit with it for a short period of time.

Do you know what emotions you are feeling that might be attached to that sensation? Sit with that vulnerability for a short period of time, then give yourself permission – this is the key here – give yourself *permission* that it's okay for you to start to heal, to heal yourself from all of this pain.

Now slowly make any of those niggly uncomfortable feelings breathe out of your body. As you do so, start to acknowledge that you are ready to move away from the left-hand side of that continuum. Get a vision in your mind of that continuum; see yourself moving along from the left-hand side of moving away, towards the right-hand side of moving towards. You don't need to see your goals or any solutions right now; you just need to give yourself permission, to tell yourself you are ready to move towards the life you want for you.

Because you are worth it.

Chapter 7
Letting Go

"What's the greater risk? Letting go of what people think – or letting go of how I feel, what I believe and who I am?"
Brené Brown

Past hurts and old injustices have a way of keeping us stuck, of holding us back, of ensuring we are unable to move forward or experience positive emotions again. Our pain may stem from people who have let us down, parents who weren't there, people who have betrayed us, the ex who cheated, the kids who bullied you, the boss who humiliated you, the person who insulted you.

Perhaps you're stuck because of the residue of your own choices, the secrets you keep about your sexual experiences, the betrayals you've made, the poor health choices you've made.

No matter where it stems from, it is an emotional quicksand that traps us at every turn, that infiltrates our thoughts, our daydreams and our dreams. It can become so ingrained that we replay it constantly and feel it within every part of our body. Our neural pathways light up to follow that path and that ongoing destructive pattern, over and over again, to our absolute detriment. Our strong urge to right these past experiences, injustices and wrongs, that can never be undone, to continually revisit our hurt and our pain, is what keeps us stuck.

It's time...

Time to acknowledge that others, and even ourselves, have caused us pain and we have chosen to continue to revisit and live with this pain. It is now time for us to give ourselves permission to move forward, once and for all, towards an alternative story, to rewrite our future and no longer let our past experiences define us or to carry them around as our identity.

Getting unstuck from this past traumatic experience means being truthful about how you feel, allowing yourself to be vulnerable and honest and raw about the emotions that come up for you.

Are you still angry? Are you frustrated? Do you want to scream and yell and punch something? Are you sad? Are you crying uncontrollably? Are you worried? Does your brain never switch off or are you completely numb, and perhaps you just don't feel anything at all?

We can often feel really stressed about the idea of letting go of these feelings, these memories, these stories we've told ourselves for so long, these beliefs, the values that we've taken on, the messages that we've taken on from others that were never ours to own, or that we have chosen to believe. We can feel really stressed because of our response in a certain situation, we feel stressed about the idea of letting it go as there can be a fear of what might happen when we do.

What will happen when you no longer have these things in your life? That lingering emotion may feel like it's the only thing that's got you through your life so far. It may feel like it's been the energetic process that's kept you moving away from the pain, that's kept you going and placing one foot in front of the other.

However, what we know is that moving beyond the pain of the past is the only way to be able to truly move forward. Let me introduce you now to a concept that is truly fascinating and, I feel, the key to enabling us to get to the core of the matter and finally let go.

There has been significant development within the field of neuroscience in the last decade in particular; this is a continually evolving area. One of the most significant things that I heard and have integrated into my ABS model was around the work of Marvin Oka and Grant Soosalu.

Oka is a behaviour modelling expert and author who claims that we actually have three brains rather than the one we have traditionally been led to believe exists. This is based on the latest scientific research. We have complex, adaptive and fully functional neural networks or 'brains' in our heart, our gut and our head.

All three brains have very distinct roles and we must understand each one in order to arrive at a point where we make better decisions. All three areas can take on information, process it, store it, and change and adapt. Ultimately, if it can learn, then it's a brain.

Head brain
This is the master of processes. It incorporates thinking, logic, reasoning, perception, analysis, how we make meaning of the world, as we see or language it and cognition. It creates narratives as well as creative new ideas, new thinking, and new perspectives (e.g .'I think ', 'I reckon', 'I understand').

Heart brain

This is where we process deep emotions, what we feel, and connections we have with others such as love, hate, or compassion. It is also where our values lie, the process of emoting, our dreams, desires and aspirations (e.g. 'I feel….').

Gut brain

This is where our intuition and our core identity lie, as well as our sense of self. It is also responsible for safety and protection, boundaries and impulse actions, as well as upholding our immune system, and also takes care of self-preservation such as the fight or flight response, as well as fear, anxiety, mobility and action (e.g. 'it takes guts', 'let's do it').

Disconnection between the three brains creates imbalance, dysfunction and conflict and restricts growth and contribution.

When we experience trauma, at least one of the three brains becomes disconnected (often the heart brain when you choose to shut off feeling and emotion). The ABS process looks to reconnect all three of the brains again as we need all of them integrated to ensure logic, reasoning and perception, new thinking and new perspectives; emotion regulation, values, dreams, desires and aspirations; and core identity and a sense of self and intuition.

The Letting Go and Forgiveness process works to reconnect the three brains and the Future Design session enables you to move forward.

Forgiveness is a gut-based issue. It is often needed because something has trespassed our boundaries and offended our safety or core identity. The gut is focused around taking action; when you are stuck, it is because of something that

Chapter 7 – Letting Go

has hit that area of identity and you are stuck in inaction. When your 'stuckness' or anger or hate is poisoning you, you need to let go, you need to take action to put it behind you so you can move forward.

By understanding the three-brain connection and how we make sense of the world, we can then engage in the journey of understanding where trauma gets stuck and why, and how to 'unstick' it and process it fully so as to reintegrate the three brains to fully communicate and to have more conscious awareness of things.

We need to open our heart *and* our mind *and* our gut, because we get a lot of neural messages from our gut response. We need to be prepared to fight the resistance that will definitely surface as we start to give ourselves permission to let go of the stuff that has kept us from moving forward, as part of who we are, for such a long period of time.

What we know is that change of any sort is uncomfortable. Ask yourself very clearly, 'Is the pain of what you're feeling now by being stuck in this emotional and physical quicksand, by being stuck where you are, is that what you want to choose to continue to feel for the rest of your life?' Or are you ready to open yourself up to being vulnerable, to writing a new story and a new beginning and a new future, to feeling positive emotions again, feelings of love, of gratitude, and of hope.

The letting-go step of the ABS model is the *most powerful part* of the entire process.

This step and the next step that follows undoubtedly have the greatest power of this entire change work. It's best done through a one-on-one, or in a group situation process in person. It is life-changing, it's transformational! There's no doubt about it. However, it isn't simple to explain.

Unfortunately I can't write it all in a book, as the change work is in the 'doing'. I would be compromising my moral and ethical principles and integrity to write the entire process down but not provide supervision and not be able to assist you with the change work that may or may not be needed.

When I first started out in this work, I gave my clients an undertaking that I would not do them any harm and I intend to uphold that, so the letting go version that is contained within this book is powerful, though it may not provide such a complete level of deep transformation on its own. It is a safe and edited version in that it will be controlled and still allow you to let go of the emotional baggage that you have held on to for all this time.

If at any stage during this process, you find yourself feeling overwhelmed with emotion, please refer to the Date Stamping process that can be found in *Appendix 3*. This process is a fantastic process that was developed by my great friend and colleague Margaret Johnson, a forensic psychologist who has specialised in trauma treatment for many years also. The Date Stamping process will ensure that any overwhelming negative emotion that occurs is very quickly settled and you return to feeling calm and safe.

If, at the conclusion of this exercise and the completion of this book, you feel that you want a deeper transformative process, then please go online to my website **www.drnataliegreen.com.au/ABSworkshops** and register for an upcoming ABS workshop at a discounted price as my gift to you for having utilised this process through purchasing the book.

Let's begin the letting go process now. Feel free to read through this process and then complete the exercise. There is also an audio version of this process available on my website that you can access at **www.drnataliegreen.com.au/ LettingGo** which will ensure you get its complete practical experience.

At the end of the last chapter we conducted a body scan where you got in touch with and tuned in to the feelings, emotions and sensations that you feel within your body. This process is about reconnecting you to the Heart and Gut brains within you and reactivating them, given they most likely have been restricted or shut down for some time as a result of your pain. I want you to do that now.

> Close your eyes, take a couple of deep breaths and slowly scan your body for any feelings that emerge, any niggly aches, pains, feelings of discomfort. Notice them, notice anywhere at all that might feel as though something is stuck within you and that it's not completely processed. Your head might feel tight, your neck, your shoulders, your chest, your stomach. Just notice it. Now, whatever they may be, bring the feelings attached to those sensations to the surface, do so naturally, then bring them to the forefront of your mind as you start to focus, just noticing them with the view of letting them go.
>
> Label them, simply for what they are. They are emotions, they are not who you are, they are separate from you, they are purely emotions.
>
> Simply observe them, don't step into them and feel them; just notice that they are there. Then move them around as if they are outside you. Notice them for what they are. Now move that sensation, that feeling, outside your body, separate from you. Does it have a shape, is it curved or spiky? Perhaps a colour: is it red, is it black?
>
> All that emotion that's outside you now, it's old stuff and it can't hurt you. Recognise what it is that you have separate from you. It's no longer part of you.

Then look more closely and recognise that there are cords leading from your body outside to that shape, that 'blob' of emotions, whatever shape or form it took, and those cords are the things that are keeping you attached to the negative thoughts, the images and the feelings.

Notice the sensation within your body as it flows along those cords. Label that emotion. Is it fear? Is it anxiety? Is it anger? Is it fear of the unknown? Fear of additional pain and hurt? Fear of failure? Again, notice it for what it is and see all the cords that are keeping you stuck from moving forward to where you want to go. Notice that if there is anger, if there are sensations that evoke fear, you don't want them there anymore. Keep that blob outside yourself and now tell yourself you're ready to move forward.

Give yourself permission to let this go, to confront these barriers that are keeping you stuck, to smash right through them. Call on your courage that you have already found as you step into your true strength of character and face those emotions head-on. Cut those cords right now, keep cutting them around you. Cut them away, and keep on cutting them to ensure that every single fibre of those cords is completely cut and gone.

There is no longer anything attached to you from within; all that negative emotion and energy is separate. Gather up all the things that were attached at the ends of those cords and bundle them together, separate from you now, and let them go. Put them into something, whether it be a rocket that blasts off, a hot air balloon, an anchor that you drop to the bottom of the sea. Take yourself through that process right now, bundling them all up and letting them go. Watch as they all disappear, never to be seen again.

Send it on its way, let it go. Completely let it go.

Chapter 7 – Letting Go

Then breathe, in and out. With every breath out, focus on all those old feelings that have gone with them, attached to those cords that you have sent on their way. Scan your body again and with every breath in, breathe in that inner peace, strength and courage as you start to live in the present, to focus on the feeling that remains as all that baggage is gone and now you are truly ready to find a way to move forward.

Well done! You are free of the negative emotions that have held you back all this time.

Chapter 8
Pain Relief

"Forgiveness is not always easy. At times, it feels more painful than the wound we suffered, to forgive the one that inflicted it. And yet, there is no peace without forgiveness."
Maryanne Williamson

Well done on taking on the Letting Go process and embracing it with everything you have! I trust that you are now feeling lighter and working on finding a level of inner peace away from where that old turmoil existed.

So many times we hear people say, 'you need to move on', 'you need to forgive and forget' – blah, blah, blah. You might think 'that's easy for them to say' or 'they've got no idea'. You might even find yourself getting angry at the very thought of forgiving someone for what they've done. Let me just say, this chapter is around helping you find pain relief. Helping you to work through a process so that you can ultimately find forgiveness.

It's not easy; indeed, it's far from easy. From experience, I know that people do what they do for whatever reason, and sometimes we just simply can't make sense of it or even begin to understand it.

I firmly believe that most people do the best they can with the resources available to them at the time. Unfortunately, though, a lot of people don't have appropriate resources they can access and sometimes it's about accepting that it's okay not to understand why someone has done something.

For many people, they have held onto their trauma, their pain or their issue for so long. As I have said, it has become a part of who they are, part of their identity even, and the idea of living without this part of them is unthinkable. They would feel fear rise within them even thinking about what it might be like not to have that as part of them and who they are, let alone the idea of forgiving the person, people or situation that created the trauma. The thought is simply far too painful to entertain.

For other people, holding onto the anger, the pain and the hurt is what fuels their fire, their motivation to continue on with their life. Indeed, it is often the only thing that gets them through, that enables them to put one foot in front of another, to simply exist.

Our own beliefs, instilled in us from a very young age, undoubtedly impact our understanding of the concept of forgiveness and what we make it mean for us.

However, what I will ask is for you to consider the concept of forgiveness as I will endeavour to define it, to try it on for yourself and see if it might be possible for you to entertain as part of the process of enabling you to have the freedom you are truly seeking. You have now managed to let go of the pain, but if you can't find forgiveness, the process will be incomplete.

There are a few sayings that really stick in my mind. One saying is: 'If you don't make peace with your past, it will keep showing up in your present'. I honestly see it happening over and over again to many people around us. Another saying that I'd like you to try on as far as forgiveness goes is: 'Forgiveness is not always easy. At times it feels more painful than the wound we suffered, to forgive the one that inflicted the hurt, and yet there is no peace without forgiveness'. And perhaps one of the most powerful ones: 'Forgive, not because they deserve forgiveness, but because you deserve peace'.

When we carry a hurt and a pain so deeply within us, we don't just carry that pain in our minds or memory, it's likely become more deeply ingrained and integrated into our body by way of emotional, physiological and physical pain and it is carried deep within us. If we keep carrying it around, it can become part of our identity and indeed our story. This is impacting the Heart and Gut brains in a negative and imbalanced way. It will impact our physical health, our immune and central nervous systems and can integrate with our entire neurology.

I ask a simple question of you: By holding onto this hurt and pain you are experiencing right now, who is winning, who is really in control of your life?

Another question: Do you think the person or thing that has inflicted your pain continues to feel as you do? Or have they seemingly gotten on with their life?

From my experience in treating thousands of clients who have presented with some sort of trauma or significant pain, the latter is usually the case in most situations.

My way of looking at forgiveness is not about forgetting that it happened, or dismissing the situation and the significance of its impact. It is ultimately about forgiving, in order to free yourself from the bitterness and all the negative emotional cords that get you down and keep you stuck, as you honestly deserve better.

The memory stays, not to be forgotten, but to be remembered as a valuable lesson. While you may not particularly recognise right now what that lesson is, the learnings will come and it will be an important part of your story that will have given you strength and courage and carried you through.

It is important to understand that forgiveness doesn't excuse their actions. But forgiveness stops their actions from destroying your heart. It takes the power away from them, once and for all, and it empowers you.

You've already completed a process aimed at letting go of negative emotions and energies, and cutting all the cords that have bound you in the past. The completion of that process comes around through forgiveness.

Let's identify what actually there is for you to forgive.

Recognise that forgiveness is a gift that you give to yourself, so that you can release all the negative energy and emotions around them. It doesn't mean that you approve of or agree with what has happened in your past. It means, however, that you are ready to release the pain in order to be able to stand in your own power again.

On a new bit of paper or in the downloaded workbook, I want you now to write down all the things that came up for you as you worked through the 'letting go' process. What is there to forgive? Who is there to forgive? Write it down, notice it, don't attach emotion to it. Just write it down as if you are just quoting facts.

Action
Transforming your trauma/pain

Turn to the *Transforming Your Trauma/Pain* Exercise in the workbook where you will find these questions to answer:

- What is the story you have grown up with/carried with you as a result of your pain?
- How has that shown up in your life?
- What is the core underlying belief within that story for you?
- What was their positive intention for themselves?
- What is there to love or be grateful for?
- What is there to forgive?

Now as I have already said, forgiveness is a gift you are going to give yourself to release your pain at the deepest possible level. Let's start with something practical: I want you to write a letter of forgiveness, not to send to anyone, purely for your own benefit right now. Writing a letter of forgiveness will help you release the negative emotions you have been carrying around for years.

Action
Forgiveness letter exercise

Here is a template right here for you to use (there is another version in the workbook for you to complete and write in). You can use the information from the Transforming Your Trauma exercise to assist you to write your Forgiveness Letter.

I forgive you, _____, for, _____
_____
I understand that you believed _____
_____.
I understand that you had a positive intention for yourself of _____.
I understand that *now* is the time for me to stand in my power.
I understand that the part of me that felt _____, _____, _____, _____, wanted to be _____, _____, _____, _____, and I am choosing to give that to myself now.
I love myself enough to let go of those old feelings so that I can give myself all of the _____, _____, _____, _____, I need.
By forgiving you I am regaining my power and I am free to be _____, _____, _____, _____.
I forgive you.
This emotional debt between us has now been settled.
I forgive you and I forgive myself. I am now free!
Signed _____

My encouragement to you would be that after you've written that forgiveness letter, you stand up and plant your feet firmly on the ground, stand up straight and strong and read it out loud as if you are speaking directly to the person who you are forgiving. When that is complete, shred it or burn it to help further let it go and complete the process fully and enable you to move on with your life.

> It's toughest to forgive ourselves. So it's probably best to start with other people. It's almost like peeling an onion. Layer by layer, forgiving others, you really do get to the point where you can forgive yourself.
> **Patty Duke**

Just to reiterate, forgive, not because they deserve forgiveness, but because you deserve peace. While the most challenging part may have seemed to be forgiving others outside yourself, it's now time to turn the focus internally.

Turn it within yourself and ask yourself the million-dollar question: 'Who is it that I *really* need to forgive?'

Who has carried the burden all this time? Who has felt and experienced all of the pain, day in and day out? Who has made choices in life based on this pain and the beliefs created out of this pain? And who is it that really needs the gift of freedom and true forgiveness right now?

That's right – it is *you*! It is time to see the forgiveness process through to completion and forgive yourself.

As another gift to you for having purchased the book, I would ask you to now go across again to the website link associated with this book (**www.drnataliegreen.com.au/Forgiveness**) and receive a copy of the free forgiveness exercise audio that will ensure that this forgiveness exercise is fully complete and integrated within you, once and for all, so you know that you have completely let go and taken the forgiveness exercise right through to completion.

> And now, again, I want you to close your eyes and take some deep, slow breaths. Focus on what's going on within your body right now. Do another body scan to ensure that your three brains are coming together and starting to work together as a team again.
>
> 1. Check in, from the tip of your head right through your body down to the tips of your toes, to see if there are any left-over emotions, any left-over niggly feelings. If there are, I want you to focus on where they are; move them around within you, recognise the shape or the form that they've taken, notice its exact colour. Focus on one area; make it a bit bigger and then shrink it really quickly. Make it really small – really, really small – make it tiny. Then let it go again, breathing it out, letting it go; place it external to you. Take some big slow deep breaths; with every breath out you breathe out all of the pain, all of the negative energy, and with each breath in, you breathe in a nice bright fulfilling energy, an energy of calm. Have it flow into your body and fill you with a sense of inner peace as you know that you are now free of all the harm that has been caused to you by others and by yourself for holding on. Check any negative emotional cords stemming from your body. Cut any of those cords and ensure they are fully and completely gone.
>
> 2. As you breathe in, I want you to focus on that inner light that has been created within you, that sense of calm within you, that positivity, that sense that you will be okay. You are now in control, you are now complete. As you breathe in that sense of calm, I want you to recognise the positive symbol of hope

and strength that sits within you. Whatever image comes to your mind that means something to you, I want you to breathe in all the positive energy of hope, strength and courage. Make that symbol as big as you want to, make it the colour that reflects that sense of strength and hope within you. Put it within you near your heart, your head, your forehead, wherever you want it to be, so you can access it at any time.

3. Know that you have it within you and with every positive thing that happens in your life, from this day onward. You top it up at the end of each day, you reflect with gratitude for every positive thing in your life and for everything that has happened that day that's positive. You allow that nice, warm, calm, comfortable feeling to flow in with every breath to get into your heart and fill up, top up, that symbol of hope, strength and courage that you have now within you, inserted and integrated deep within.

4. Notice all of the positive resources that come with that belief, that despite having been through all of this, you've been given a gift and this gift has allowed you to be stronger than you ever were before. Now bring that feeling of hope, of calm, of strength and courage; have it expand and grow bigger and stronger. How good does that feel now? Complete your body scan and notice the calm and comfortable feelings that are now within you, free of all the cords of negativity, negative emotions. Know that you are in control of you, you are in control of your destiny.

5. What do you notice about yourself now? How do you feel? You can even test it out by going back to a time when you felt that old negative emotion. Think about it and notice the change within you right now. You have now given yourself the gift of true forgiveness and are well on the way to being free.

Chapter 9
Begin Again

"Let nothing dim the light that shines from within."
Maya Angelou

So now you've done the hardest parts, you've identified your issues and your challenges, you've acknowledged their actual impact on you and you've owned it. You've processed what has happened, you've let go of the negative emotions that have been caused and created for you as a result of your experience and you've forgiven those at the source of your pain and suffering, as well as, most importantly, yourself for having held onto all those negative responses and emotions and the impact of these for all this time.

Now it's time to begin again and create the person you wish to be with a 'going forward' motivation in your life. This person will be the new you, with some old beliefs, mindset and identity that you choose to maintain, the parts of you that are resourceful and served you through giving you strength, and the values that you wish to continue with that have been positive in your journey thus far.

Firstly, let's start by giving yourself *permission*, permission to be able to be who you desire to be, free of the burdens and constraints of the past. As you do this, let's run through the process that by now you're very familiar with, the body scan, to ensure that you are comfortable with this now.

Conduct that body scan within yourself. As you give yourself permission to be able to become the person you choose to be, take notice of what's going on within your body as you do this. Notice if there is anyone whose feelings you're concerned about if you become the new you. If so, then you can follow the process in *Appendix 4 (Negative Energy Release and Permission to Move Forward Process)* to release the negative energy around that, and create a new statement that you are comfortable with that will allow you to give permission to be you.

Secondly, values are principles or standards of behaviour that we judge to be important in life. They can also be known as moral principles or ethics. They'll be a major influence on our behaviour or attitudes. They serve as broad guidelines across all situations; they almost steer us like a moral compass. When our values are not met or have been compromised by others, or we are in situations that are out of our control, we can feel as though our values are in significant conflict.

It's time to get back in touch with your core values, or establish some new ones that are non-negotiable for you and that will assist you by serving as your own moral compass.

Action
Values exercise

Ask yourself the question: What is important to you now that you are free of all your negative energy? What is important to you in the context of your relationships, your health, your career, and for you personally?

If you are unsure how to answer this, refer to the sample Values List that I have included here. This is not an exhaustive list, and obviously many people have other values founded in culture, spiritual belief, ritual, tradition and family upbringing.

Accomplishment
Acceptance
Accountability
Accuracy
Adaptability
Adventure
Beauty
Calm (inner peace)
Challenge
Change
Cleanliness
Collaboration
Commitment
Communication
Community
Competence
Competition
Concern (for others)
Continuous improvement
Cooperation
Coordination
Courteousness
Creativity
Decisiveness
Democracy
Discipline
Discovery
Efficiency
Equality
Excellence
Fairness
Faith
Family
"Family values"
Financial Security

Flexibility
Freedom
Friendship
Fun
Genuineness
Good Will
Gratitude
Hard work
Harmony
Honesty
Honour
Independence
Innovation
Integrity
Justice
Knowledge
Leadership
Love or Romance
Loyalty
Merit
Money
Openness
Orderliness
Non-violence
Patience
Perfection
Persistence
Personal Growth
Pleasure
Positive attitude
Power
Practicality
Preservation
Privacy
Problem Solving

Professionalism
Prosperity
Punctuality
Quality of work
Regularity
Resourcefulness
Respect (of & for others)
Responsiveness
Results-oriented
Safety
Satisfying others
Security
Self-sacrifice (a giving of self)
Self-reliance (a reliance on self)
Simplicity
Skill
Speed
Spirituality
Stability
Status
Strength
Systemization
Teamwork
Timeliness
Tolerance
Tradition
Tranquility
Trust
Truth
Unity
Variety
Vitality
Wealth
Willingness
Wisdom
Youthfulness

> For example, my top values are around honesty and integrity. If I'm in a situation where I feel someone is not being truthful or honest or is being deceitful, my warning radar starts to signal to me.
>
> I feel conflicted, I'm compromised and I choose not to engage in that situation, or I extract myself from it as soon as I can as it simply isn't a fit for me.
>
> Of course, I don't always get it right. It's not about being perfect, but I'm certainly more aware of it now and as a result I enjoy better relationships with friends and colleagues and I distance myself from people who are presenting a values conflict for me.
>
> What I want you to do right now is come up with your top five values, using the values list provided. These can serve as your general guide to who you are and who you wish to become.

Thirdly, in order to really begin moving forward with the new you, whether we like it or not, we live in a society where there are rules.

We often unknowingly and at an unconscious level make our own rules, rules that we perceive to be true based on our own values, beliefs, identity, environment and experiences.

In order to ensure that we are truly stepping into our own power and that we are in control of ourselves in the new world, we need to examine the world rules that we will set for ourselves.

Let's take a look at it in this way (opposite page).

Chapter 9 – Begin Again

Old World vs New World

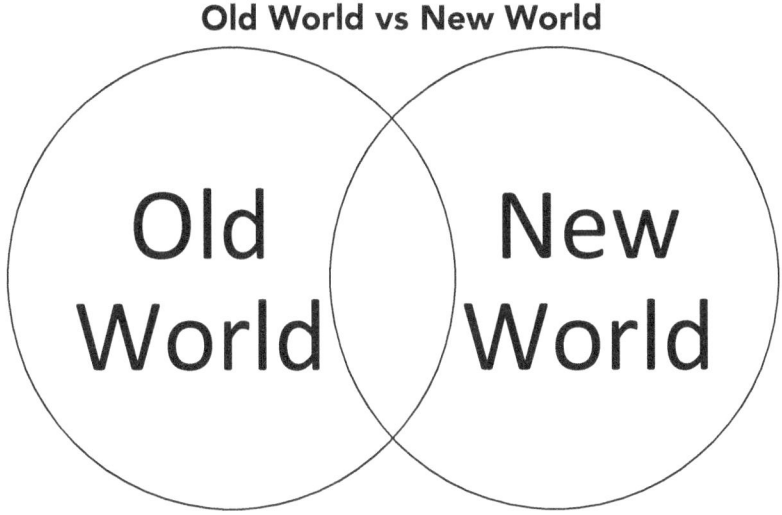

We look at the way you've thought, felt and behaved when the baggage from your past has dominated your life. That is what we term the *old world*. Then we look at the way in which you would think, feel and behave when you no longer carry that internal baggage around with you, having let it go completely and severed its ties. That's what we refer to as the *new world*.

What thoughts, feelings and behaviours ruled your world when the old world rules were followed constantly? They can be things like, 'I'm scared', 'I'm not good enough', 'I can't cope', 'others are in control', 'I'm a bad person', 'I have no control', 'it's not worth trying'.

Then I want you to think about, as a result of your old experiences, what strengths you have drawn upon or what gifts you have been given. Be really clear on which world rules, which values, behaviours and identity you wish to take on. These become your new world rules.

They can be things like, 'I'm happy with who I am', 'I make the decisions', 'I am in control of me', 'I take responsibility', 'I allow myself to feel', 'I am safe', 'I am grateful', 'I am courageous'.

Action
New world rules
The action I want you to take is to write down on a piece of paper what your new world rules are. Write them down and commit to them. Do that now.

I want you to know that you will not get it right a hundred per cent of the time; you are a work in progress. But as long as you maintain your awareness around who you are and your values and beliefs, and the rules that you wish to abide by in your new world, you will be moving towards who you are looking to become.

Never forget that you are worth it!

Chapter 10
Future Design

"Though no one can go back and make a brand new start, anyone can start from now and make a brand new ending."
Carl Bard

In order to live a life of choice and happiness, one must start with the end in mind. In order to have a clear direction in where you are heading, it's important to set goals. I know some of you will think, 'I've done lots of goal setting work before. I'm over it, it doesn't work', or you just do it in your head and think, 'Yeah, I'll work towards that'. What we know from experience with the thousands of clients that I've worked with over the years, is that setting clear goals and having plans to work towards them, makes you much more likely to achieve your desired outcome.

There are two well known university studies that are often quoted, one done by Yale University in 1953 and the other reportedly replicated by Harvard Business School in 1979, which analysed their graduating class and then followed up on them years later. Both studies demonstrated that 84% of the students had set no goals for themselves, 13% had set written goals but had no concrete plans and 3% had both written goals and concrete plans. At the follow-up, the group in the 13% category had made twice as much money as the others and the group of 3% had reportedly made ten times as much. These studies have been quoted for years. Though many have tried to debunk them over the years, what is clear from multiple studies now is that those who set goals and have clear plans to reach them are overall more successful.

Goal setting is important. The majority of you may have heard of a process used in goal setting called SMART goals: Specific, Measurable, Achievable, Realistic and Time-based or Timely. To ensure that they come to fruition, it's important to write them in the first person as if they are now.

It's certainly helpful to use this process and I would encourage you to do that. There is a SMART goal sheet included in the downloadable workbook. I suggest you give that a go to be clear on what sort of goals you would like to set for yourself into the future.

However, I will also introduce you to another few exercises that can also integrate a future vision and identity for you that will stick with you in the longer term and will be more integrated in your neural pathways and neurology.

It is really important as you grow and reach for new heights, free of all the things that have held you back in the past, that you are comfortable with the new you. It's important that you have ways to check in and see how far you've come. It is also important that you get clarity as to exactly what it is that you want, because until you have clarity about what you're moving towards, you may well find that you're still in a 'moving away' motivated state.

So this process will allow you to design the future you desire, to be clear on what you want and to enable you to feel in control of yourself and your future. The choice to create who you want to be and the life you want to live is essential, especially when you've come from where you've come from.

Action
Design your home

What I want you to do now is to take out another piece of paper or go to the page in your workbook marked Future Design. We're going to become draftspeople, house designers and architects.

On the left hand side of the page when you align the page horizontally, I want you to draw your old life as a house plan. Draw it as it was under the rules of your old world. I want you to draw on that house plan every room that made up your home.

In your house, I want you to include a room for every part of your life that was taken up in some way; for example, if trauma kept you stuck, stopped you going outside, stopped you mingling with other people, and impacted your relationships, then you're going to have a pretty big room in your house which constitutes a trauma room.

Your house (or even shack) may be one that's pretty run down and ramshackle. It may have a big trauma room as the main room in your house.

It may have other rooms that include children, your partner; you may have a room that included work. There might be only a tiny little room there for sleep, there might be a little tiny room for activities or hobbies that you like to do, there might be a room for anger, there might be a room for alcohol.

You write down all the rooms in your house based on the main activities that filled your life previously, prior to you engaging in the ABS process.

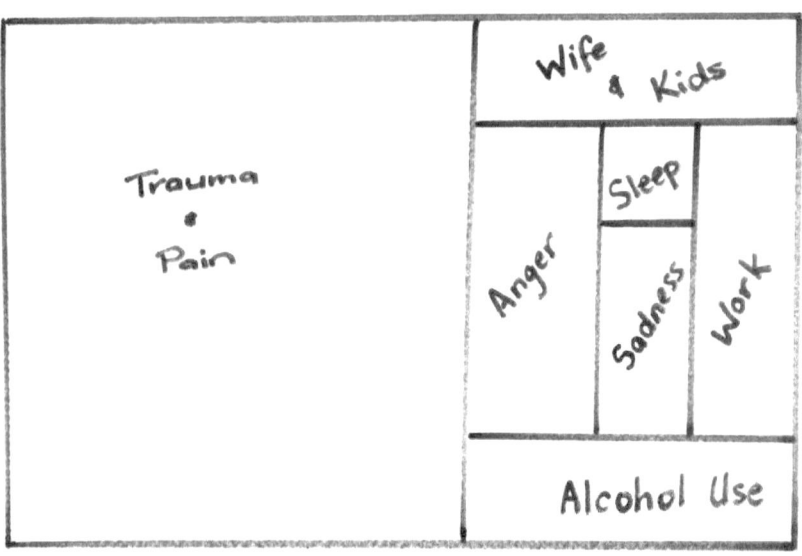

Then on the other side of the page I want you to draft your new house plan as you want it to be, now that you've let go of all the negative emotions and the old baggage that had taken up so much of your time and after you've engaged in forgiveness. Build the new house, make it your home. It might be a mansion, it might be a little tiny house, but fill it with all the things, the activities you want to do, the relationships you want in your life, all the things that you want in your house.

Please note that it's not a house plan as it is right now. It's a house plan that will include the skills that you have right now, with the house that you want to build in the future; it will be a work in progress. You might include rooms for family, for connection, for relationships, for good communication, for time with your partner, time with your kids, time with other family members. You might include a room for working, for activities, for sport, for things that you used to engage in, that you'd ceased because you didn't feel

Chapter 10 – Future Design

you were able to continue with them. You might add on verandahs for time with friends, for socialising, new trainings, new future things that you have always wanted to do but you've held yourself back from doing. You might even write a book, you might engage in something you didn't think was possible prior to engaging in the ABS system.

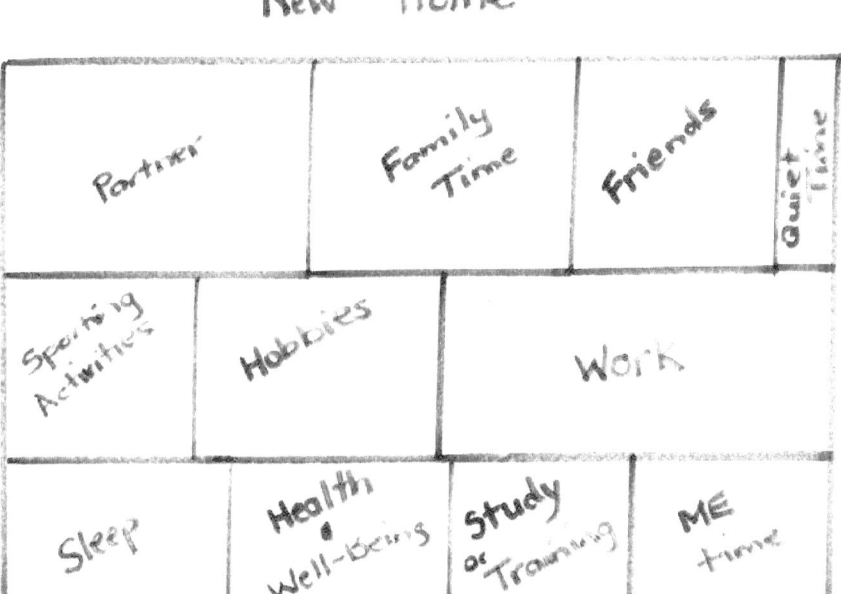

Now I want you to continue to draw the house plan as you envisage your home might be. Have a look at the house you've designed. Research combined with experience would indicate that people who have a good sense of self, self-esteem, self-worth and who live with a greater amount of peace in their lives include three main areas in their lives to ensure they have greater happiness and inner peace. They have meaningful relationships, opportunities for growth and community connection and contribution. If you have integrated all three of those areas, then your house is solid. If there's one missing, just add in another room in your house. Design it so you're covering all three of the areas that we know will help you to have a greater sense of self-worth and value.

What we also know from years and years of research, work and practical integration is that human beings process information in three main ways. Visually, they process things through seeing, through imagining, and through visualising them. They also process things from an auditory perspective. They do this by listening, processing things through sounds, through making sense of it through their minds. They also process things kinaesthetically, through touch, through sensory avenues, through not only feeling but also emotions (they are also incorporated in the kinaesthetic component).

What we know when we're looking to design our future, to have the greatest chance of happiness, peace and greater sense of freedom, is that if we can visualise our life, and connect what we see to a kinaesthetic feeling (i.e. integrating our Head Brain with our Heart Brain), this vision can trick the brain into not knowing what's real and what's not yet real. So if we can create a vision of how we want things to be, and it evokes feelings and positive emotions in the process and our brain sees it often enough, it gets the message that this will become our reality.

Action
Vision board
The next exercise for this chapter is therefore for you to create a vision board. Cut out pictures that have significant meaning for you, write words, do whatever it is that will enable you to connect to it from a Heart, Head and Gut brain perspective. Get yourself a nice bit of cardboard and paste the pictures onto it.

Kinaesthetically, you can feel it, you can touch it, and as you feel it, you're emotionally connected to it. You bring it to life in a board so that your brain will start to work towards that and bring that vision to reality and fruition. I always have

Chapter 10 – Future Design

all my clients in all my mentoring programs create a vision board early on, so they are really clear on who they are, what they believe in and where they are heading. It's a true representation of the version of you that you are creating and there is a far greater chance of that vision becoming a reality. Put it up in your room, in front of your desk, wherever it is that you'd prefer, so that you see it every single day. It's there and it becomes integrated into you.

Sample Vision Board

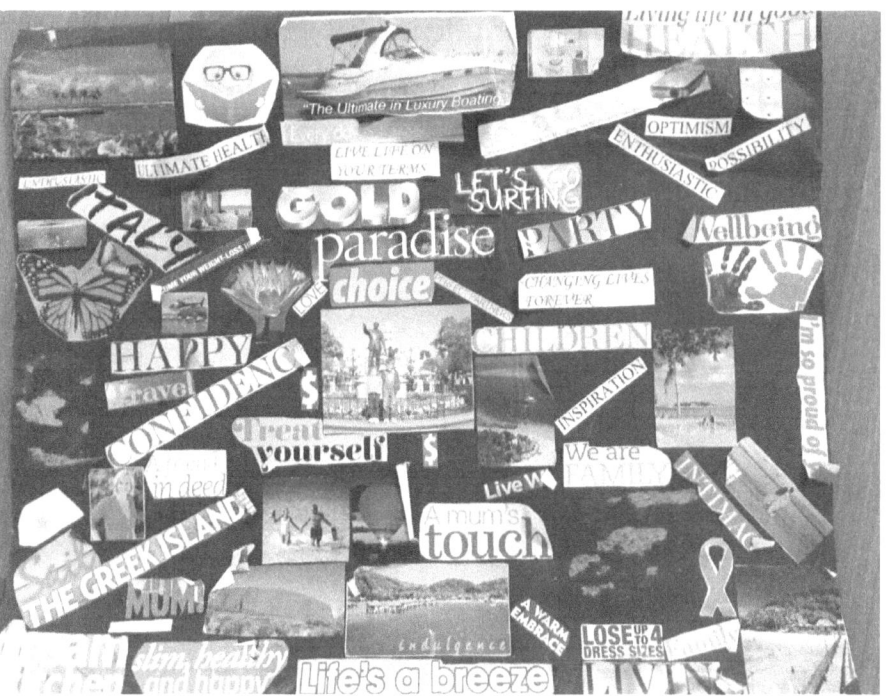

Action
Create your visualisation and bring it to life

Now you can feel and see the future you're designing. We now need to integrate that last component, which is the auditory component. What I would like you to do is to create your own visualisation. The best way to do this is for you to use your own voice, on your iPhone or smart phone or whatever recording device you have. It doesn't have to be a great, big, long visualisation; you can just talk through all the things on your vision board. But what I want you to do is to bring your future to life. You can talk about the rooms in your house plan, all the items on your vision board, but ensure that you describe very accurately for your visualisation, what you see, describing all the colours on there, the people in your life, who you're sharing it with, what you're experiencing with them, how they make you feel, how they feel when they are with the new you, and who you are choosing to be, what choices you make – all of those things. Create your own visualisation, write it and record it.

I want you to think big, to believe in yourself as you grow and reach for these new heights, knowing that you can achieve the best version of you that you want.

You're worth it.

Chapter 11
Newfound Freedom

"Our ultimate freedom is the right and power to decide how anybody or anything outside ourselves will affect us."
Stephen Covey

For so long you've experienced the negative impact of your trauma and pain. You've felt enslaved and overwhelmed by how it evolved and infiltrated and controlled every part of your life.

Now you've worked through what has happened and completely let it go. You've forgiven those who created your pain and, most importantly, forgiven yourself for having held onto it all for so long, restricting your life.

You've looked at who you are, deep at the core, as a result of your experiences, and allowed yourself to imagine who it is you can become. You've looked at what rules you can choose to set and establish in your new world and what rules no longer need to exist for you. And you have given yourself permission to move forward and design the future you've only ever dreamt of. Now you've even designed your own house and life plan that ultimately ensures personal growth, meaningful relationships and community connection as part of your life.

To look at a bit more of the self-work, we move to the seventh step of the ABS model, that of freedom.

Now I want you to see your Ideal Self, the version of you that you now hold, without all the emotional baggage, the version of you that you are looking to become. I want you to ensure that your Ideal Self can exist in a world with your new world rules, your core values and beliefs and the amazing qualities you now bring with you as a result of having let go of the burden of your past.

Then I want you to check in with your Actual Self as you are now, without your pain, with the knowledge that you are a work in progress and that's okay, as you are doing the best you can with the resources available to you right now.

Identify what other people's standards you will choose to live up to, and their rules and expectations for you or for the world that you live in, that you will choose to place upon, or incorporate into, yourself. This is the Ought Self part of you that we have discussed in an earlier chapter.

It's really important that you ensure that they are no longer misaligned, that the Ideal Self is a little beyond your Actual Self as far as your goals, your expectations and your desires. Most of all, ensure that they are realistic as you work towards maintaining a balance between all three parts of yourself.

Maintaining minimal self-discrepancy, as well as clear core values and identity, will set you well and truly on your path to newfound freedom. If we are able to have all three components of ourselves aligned, there is less emotional, physiological and psychological pain and discomfort and we are more likely to feel we are on a true path to freedom.

Check in regularly to ensure that those versions of self are in alignment. Also check in at least on a monthly basis to determine that your house plan is incorporating more of the new house plan, the mansion that you've created, rather than the little shack of pain and past rooms that weren't serving you. The responsibility is on you to check in at least monthly to ensure you are maintaining the huge gains you have made.

Another great exercise to enable you to do this is what we call the wheel of life.

Action
The wheel of life exercise

The wheel of life is a great exercise and tool to help you create more balance and success in your life. It is often a great foundation exercise in goal setting and creating a future vision.

The action I want you to take for this chapter is to complete the wheel of life exercise that is located within the downloadable workbook. Be honest and use the scoring system from 0 to 10 to look at where you sit in all those roles of your life in respect to relationships, career, family, physical health and socially. Are you looking after you, and are you communicating appropriately with others? Are you taking on board your new values, beliefs, and identity, in all those areas of your life?

Rate yourself properly and honestly from 0 to 10 and see if the wheel of life would turn and roll along for you in the direction that you desire. Would it be a nice, smooth ride or would it be a really bumpy ride where you've got the metal scraping through and feeling like you're on a really rocky road, like you've been on in the past? It's up to you and if you find that one of those components or one area of your life or of the house plan is not living up to the standards that you've set for yourself as part of your Actual versus Ideal Self, then please focus some energy on a daily basis into that component of your life so that the ride becomes smoother.

You now have several tools that will enable you to revise your progress and keep yourself in check. In order to secure the amazing changes you have already made and integrate them as fully as possible within your neurology, let's do one last exercise to integrate the three brains and enable you to see how things can be for you, to engage your creative new thinking and perspective, process your emotions and connect to them fully to your values, dreams and desires, as well as fully integrate your sense of self, your core identity and get you to trust in your intuition again.

This connection will enable you to have the balance and function you desire in your future and ensure you to feel safe and whole again.

Action
Future vision exercise
And now let's do a future vision exercise where you look through your own eyes and see your Actual Self exactly as you are, having achieved your goal, your health goal, your relationship goal, your career, your financial goal and realising that you have achieved the success that you desired in this area exactly as you wanted for yourself.

Notice what you are wearing; see yourself and notice who's there with you. See what you are seeing, hear what you are hearing, all the noises around you, and feel the feelings deep within you. Notice how wonderful it feels. Hear exactly what you are saying to yourself. Notice the attitudes, the beliefs and the values you have used to get there to achieve this and take a snapshot of this very moment in your life.

Just sit with it for a moment, breathe in all of it, every part of it, feel it through every part of your body. You can feel the energy coursing through your veins, the warmth and the glow of that inner peace, right through your body. See it, see everything around you, as you integrate it fully and completely within yourself. It's part of you and your identity and who you have become.

Notice every component of it. Allow yourself to place that snapshot that you have taken with absolute clarity out in front of you, ahead of you, into your future. Notice the action steps you've taken to get there and what knowledge you've learnt about yourself along the way. What skills, what knowledge and tools did you learn to achieve this goal?

Sit with that, watch it as it is secured in your future, at that certain place in time, wherever and whenever that may be. Breathe it in and enjoy the amazing feeling that courses through you as if right through your veins, incorporated in every fibre of your being as you know with absolute certainty that you will attain that future for you.

And as you come right back to now in the current time, notice the milestones along the way that supported this goal and notice your attitude as you are committed right through to seeing this thing to completion. Now stop off at tomorrow on your timeline, and notice the next steps you must take to achieve this goal and then come gradually right back to now.

Action

What are your next three steps?

Your task for the last part of this chapter is to write down exactly what your next three action steps will be that will confidently take you right through to experiencing all that you have become and move you into the future so you see all the steps you need to take to get to achieve the milestones and reach your desired outcome.

The field of NLP has so much to offer in so many areas, and one of the areas that I love to bring in with my clients is that of the Neurological Levels or Logical Levels of Change. This is a concept that was developed by Robert Dilts, a leader in this field who I was privileged enough to see speak and deliver workshops in the United States on several occasions.

The concept was based on the initial work of Gregory Bateson, an anthropologist who suggested there were logical levels of learning, change and communication; however Dilts went on to develop it further and developed the Neurological Levels of Change. There are six levels that influence and shape our relationships and interactions in the world. I believe it is important to understand these concepts when we are undergoing such major change work in our lives.

Chapter 11 – Newfound Freedom

What we know is that all the levels are inter-connected and each level functions by integrating and operating upon the level beneath it. Additionally, change or activity at any particular level will also influence the level above it. If we have the skills or capabilities to do something, but we are experiencing difficulty at a specific level, that is, for some reason we continue to be stuck and unable to do what we desire, we can go to the level directly above or below it and address that to make the change we need. What we know, however, is that if we address the level above it, we are likely to get a change that has a greater impact and flow on effect at a deeper level.

This is really useful to know when you have to do some problem-solving. Look at which logical level the problem seems to be represented or 'stuck' at. Instead of working at that specific level of the problem, like most of us do when trying to make changes, it is important to realise that in order to solve the problem all we need to do is go to a different level.

If we stay at the same level, the only change we can make is to change at that particular level, whereas by shifting levels the solution to the problem becomes obvious with less effort.

For example, if you are working on something, yet each time you attempt it you fall short for some reason, you could train to develop additional skills or you could think, 'I know I actually do have the skill or capability to do this as I've done it before'. But the problem may actually stem from the beliefs/values level. Therefore, if you make a change at the belief/values level you can remove the blockage very quickly and can do a much better job at the capability level.

What I really love about this is that, to ensure that change is integrated at as deep a level within you as it can be, we want to integrate it neurologically wherever possible.

Environment
This is the *where*. The foundation is in the physical environment, what you can see, hear and touch. Is there something in your environment that prevents you from doing what you want to do (e.g. work, home, family, community etc.)?

Behaviours
This is the *what*. It includes behaviours and physical actions. Is it a problem based on the things that you are doing?

Capabilities/skills
This is *how* you do something. Is there a problem with what you're capable of doing or not doing (e.g. motivation, physically impossible, don't have skills set)?

Beliefs/values
This is *why* you do something. Your beliefs or values can either enhance your capabilities or limit them. This occurs at a deeper level within you.

Identity
This is at the *who* level. It involves who you are and is much deeper at the core than a belief.

Mission/spirit
This is *for whom/for what* and is something beyond you. It is around your purpose. When these are aligned, we can bring our vision into action.

By utilising the Logical Levels model we can also engage in reintegrating the three brains and reconnecting the head, heart and gut.

Chapter 12
New Normal

"Your time is limited, so don't waste it living someone else's life."
Steve Jobs

As we move into this final chapter we can look back. You've carried your old burden for so long so this new you trying to live in a new world with new rules can feel a bit strange, a bit weird – let's face it, a little uncomfortable to begin with. But it's just like anything new. It takes practice and a belief in yourself that you can do it and that you deserve to be happy and free of all that old stuff and junk that was weighing you down.

It will take some time to adjust to your new reality, your new 'normal'. So give yourself the gift of patience and time. Test yourself on a daily basis by living in the present moment and allowing yourself to make choices, to gradually make decisions and to experience the new you and celebrate who you are becoming.

If you notice any components of sadness, which you feel may be heading to depression, you can check in and know that you're probably focusing back on living in the past. The past is done; you have moved beyond that.

If you find that there are symptoms of anxiety creeping in, then you're likely living in the future. You're worrying about what may or may not even happen. Let's look to living in the now, to experiencing the present and the peace that this will bring with it.

As you increase your skills and your ability to live your life with your new values, your new beliefs and your identity and the absolute clarity around who you are, and you live with understanding that you can make choices within the framework that you have set for yourself, your confidence will undoubtedly grow.

I encourage you to check in on your progress on a regular basis, at a minimum three months, preferably on a more regular basis of at least once every month, especially in the beginning as you strengthen the muscle to step into your power and integrate this new version of you.

Know that the people in your life may notice changes and not understand why or who you are, so be clear with them, hold your ground and be really strong with your boundaries.

Know your non-negotiables, get good at saying no when you need to and let go of negative emotions, if and when they surface.

Review your house plan every month and make sure that you are furnishing every room and holding your structure firm. Nourish yourself, feed yourself with positive energy, affirmations and encouragement and gratitude on a daily basis and keep working towards completing your basic structure and strong foundation.

Do renovations if and when needed in your house, though ensure you meet personal growth, meaningful relationships and connections throughout your house structure to make sure you have a strong foundation.

Chapter 12 – New Normal

Another area I'm extremely passionate about, that I insist you practise to really hold the key to true freedom, is self-care.

It's the old story of you being on a plane and the airhostess runs through her usual safety drill about life jackets and oxygen masks. She very clearly informs us that we fasten our own oxygen mask first. In other words, we need to look after ourselves, so that we are fully capable of looking after others.

One of my all-time favourite quotes is: 'You can't pour from an empty vessel'. Take heed of this and practise this on a daily basis. Engage in regular self-care activities that refresh and replenish you and refill your vessel.

This is not selfish; instead, it is sound healthcare. Engaging in such regularly sets you up for success, for good health emotionally, psychologically and physically and ultimately for true freedom, so you can be the master of your own destiny.

See *Appendix 5* for a list of self-care activities that you should engage in on a regular basis. Give yourself permission to look after you.

We've already talked about life being full of ups and downs; a lot of this is certainly outside our control. As we've discovered, we can only control our responses to things, and how we choose to manage these reactions is completely up to us. A good reminder of this is the picture over the page that demonstrates that there is clear choice involved in responding.

Key to Freedom

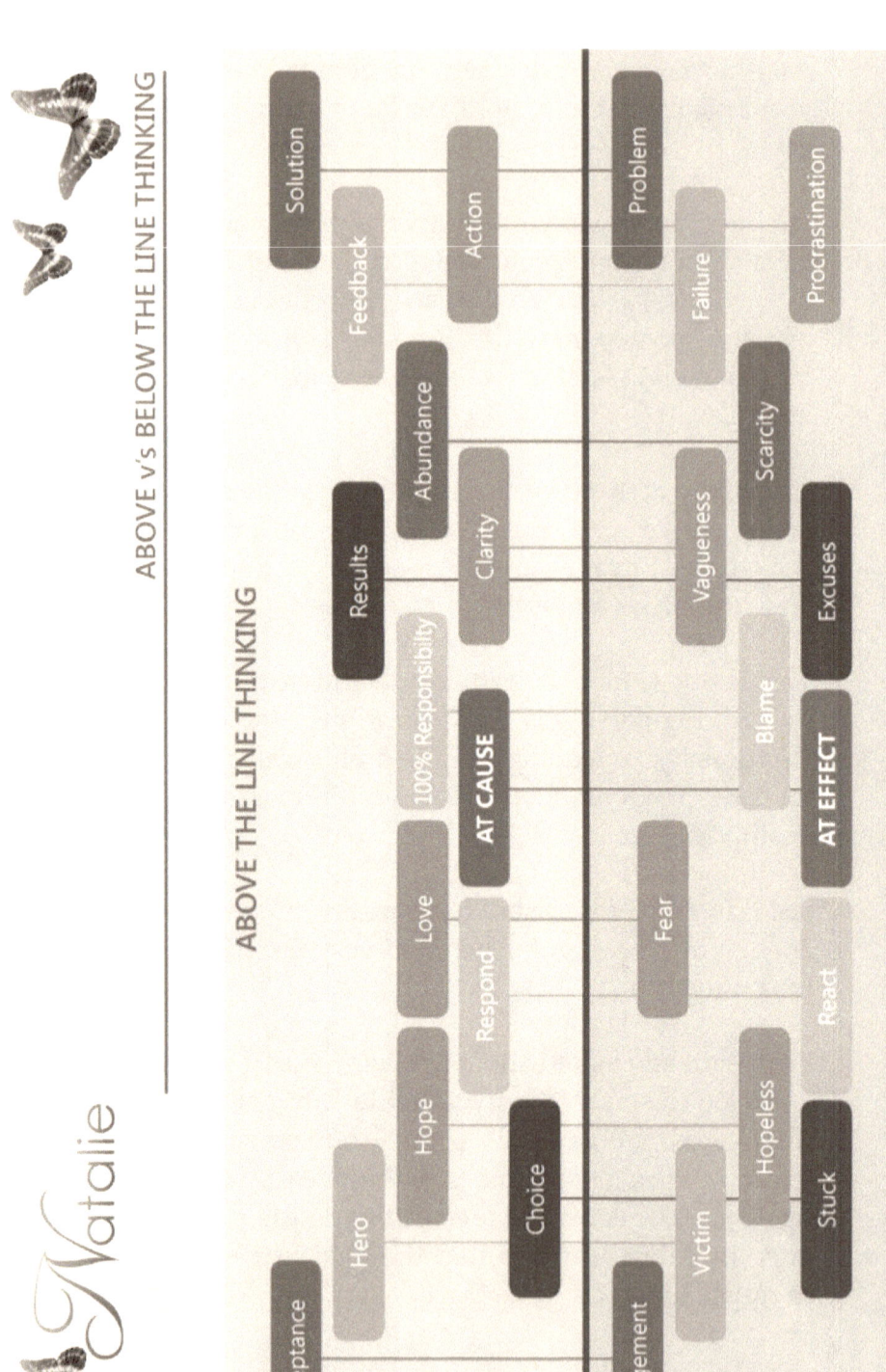

Chapter 12 – New Normal

I absolutely love this illustration; it utilises the concept of being 'At Cause' or 'At Effect'. There are two very clear ways of thinking and approaching things in our lives. We can operate 'Above The Line' with our thinking, which means we are coming from a positive mindset and we are *responding* to things that happen in our lives or we can operate 'Below The Line' with our thinking, which means we are coming from a negative mindset and we are *reacting* to things that happen in our lives.

This very clearly shows that when we are in that 'below the line' way of thinking, we get caught up in pain, in sadness, in negative thinking and we are living our life at what we call 'effect'. We often feel like things just happen to us and we are helpless as a result.

However, if we are to have the life that we plan for ourselves, that we now feel we deserve, we need to spend the majority of our time in the 'above the line' thinking.

If you notice that you slip back down below the line, identify specifically where in this diagram you are operating from and follow, from this area that you identify with, along the line right back up to the thing at the exact opposite end. This will guide you in knowing what action you can take to being back in control. For example, if you're feeling like things have happened and you're a bit of a victim, look at the exact opposite of that, which is about being a hero, and look at 'How can I be a hero in my own story in this situation? What do I need to do?'

There are so many clues all the way through this book. The answer is there. The answer is already within you. Step into your own shoes as a hero, look through the hero's eyes; you own the hero's journey, you have written the hero's journey. Feel empowered, stand up in your shoes, recognise that it's a perfect fit. Live and walk the life of the hero.

In *Appendix 6*, you will see an emotional hierarchy (developed by Pearson and Haemmerle for the DSR training I completed). These are the negative and strongest emotions that can sometimes take hold of us. These are the emotions that we must identify with to recognise that they are happening within us and it is time to work again through our 'letting go' process. If you are experiencing any of those negative emotions in the categories of anger, sadness, fear or guilt or are embarrassed or hurt or disempowered, then those emotions, if they've crept in, could have you at risk of engaging in 'below the line' thinking and behaviours.

If you notice these things rising again, you now have the ABS system. Go right back to step 1. Ensure that the awareness is there, label the issue, label the negative emotion, as awareness is key. Then move to step no. 2, which is around acceptance. Accept that it exists within you at that very time and then engage in the 'letting go' process again.

Follow the 'letting go' process through completely, process the challenge, and go through the forgiveness exercises. Come through the other side and know that you can move yourself through to 'above the line' thinking at any time. You can easily and effortlessly let go of things that previously would have become overwhelming, and would have held you back. You are now in control of your own life.

Appendix 1 contains a symptom checklist at the back of this book. If you notice that you are seeing more of these symptoms and emotions sneaking back in, or your house feels as though it's not structurally sound any more (e.g. a wall might have caved in or the veranda might have fallen off), go right back through the book, run yourself step by step right through the ABS process.

You can do this over and over again, as life is undoubtedly full of ups and downs. The more often you do it, the more

Chapter 12 – New Normal

efficient and effective you become at it, and the process is very quick and efficient. If you feel things are stuck and you need to engage yourself in the 'letting go' process and forgiveness, ensure that you then complete your body scan to ensure the process has gone right through to completion and you are free again. Disentangle any cords or negative emotions and let them go completely.

Understand fully what is yours to own and what no longer belongs to you and what never did belong to you in the first place.

Then close the lid on that box within your brain and seal it shut so you are in control of if or when it is opened.

If you notice a problem you are struggling to solve, then refer to the Logical Levels. Identify the level you are stuck at, go to the level above that and frame a question using the prompts provided at that level to help you get unstuck again.

As you become more competent and confident in the ABS process, you will note the efficiency with which you can identify the issue, let it go and forgive others and yourself across any context.

The ABS process of letting go arose out of a trauma situation and my own need to expedite things for my clients, as I found it too difficult watching them sit with their pain for so long, knowing I could help them more efficiently. This coupled with my own trauma experience sealed the deal for me, knowing I could apply this to myself in several contexts and feel so much more at peace within. I then realised it could be applied across so many contexts.

The ABS system and process can be applied to one-off traumas, it can be applied to relationships that may have domestic violence involved, or just relationships where you feel it is too difficult to move on for whatever reason. It can be applied to sexual assault victims who want to reclaim their lives and their power and to move forward again.

It can be applied to people with chronic health issues who are sick of feeling controlled by their condition, who want to let go of the loss of control, to regain the power within themselves and heal themselves as much as they can to feel whole again. It can be used for people who want to get to the root cause of why they struggle with their weight, to let go of the old version of themselves and re-establish the healthy version of themselves again.

It can be used for people in business who aren't having the success they believe they should have; no matter what they seem to do, they're still not profitable, they're not running the businesses they like, they're not coping with the staff as they desire and ultimately they're just not happy in their career. It can be applied to financial issues, letting go of old money beliefs that have been handed down from past generations, clearing those beliefs so they can establish their new family money legacy and feel true freedom and thrive.

As you can see, the ABS model has multiple applications. If there is any part of your wheel of life that feels out of whack, or if you're riding on a rusty rim, revisit it, clear any barriers and let go of those older emotions, beliefs and issues that are holding you back, once and for all.

Thank you again for joining me on my mission to make a bigger difference in the world, to assist people to let go of the past that has been causing them so much pain and holding them back for so long. Now it is time for us to really get this out there and for us to inform therapists and clinicians and professionals about the ABS model. They too can be trained in the ABS model from a therapeutic standpoint so they can deliver the deeper transformations that the one-on-one therapy can provide, through the Letting Go and Forgiveness stages of the ABS Model. More information on this for professionals can be found on the website link www.drnataliegreen.com.au/therapisttrainings.

Remember, you are the most important person in your life and you deserve to be happy and feel fulfilled and to experience true freedom and to thrive. You now hold the Key to Freedom, so go forward and control your own destiny and shine like the diamond you are in the world.

Afterword

"Character cannot be developed in ease and quiet. Only through experience of trial and suffering can the soul be strengthened, ambition inspired, and success achieved."
Helen Keller

As we've already reviewed in the last chapter, you've now gone through the entire seven-step ABS process. You've carried your old burden for so long but you've now learnt a process that has enabled you to let it all go, to actively practise forgiveness and release all of the negative energy and emotional baggage that has been weighing you down all this time; to create your new identity with absolute clarity and confidence and to be clear on your values, your beliefs and then to integrate all of these into who you are moving towards becoming, so as to live the life that you were always destined to live.

As you move forward in your journey and no longer feel that emotional burden of all that baggage weighing you down, and you activate the new you and integrate it into all of the components of your life and see, hear and feel the results as they become ingrained as a part of you, I ask that you don't lose sight of where you have come from, so you can celebrate the huge achievements that you've made and celebrate the new you as you start to thrive.

For years I've seen people seek treatment but so many have continued to stay stuck. I've seen and heard their pain and wanted to be able to do more. As you know, I've put together all my years of experience to develop this model. I know the ABS system works because I've done it with hundreds upon hundreds of clients, with absolute, complete, transformational outcomes over and over again.

I know this process works and I'm absolutely passionate about now taking this model out to the world. It's my mission to change more lives, to enable so many more people who have experienced all types of trauma, of hurt, of pain, who are continuing to suffer in living their lives or simply existing as they thought that was the only possible option for them.

I want to get this model out there in the world and help more people to make a bigger difference, so that people everywhere can live the life they were destined for. So they can be who they want to be and thrive, rather than live to survive. I simply can't stay silent any more – I want to help people let go of whatever it is that's been holding them back. I believe with all my heart that this model can truly enable people to thrive.

I know a lot of people will read this book, will hear about this model and they still won't do anything. There are many reasons for that. For some, they like being the victim, there's more in it for them to stay stuck. But I really hope that that's not you. If my words have had any impact on you at all and you have taken action, you may just need a little bit of tweaking. If you want even more assistance to live the life you truly desire, then there is a way you can reach out to me.

Please contact me on my e-mail address at drnat@drnataliegreen.com.au.

Chapter 9 – Afterword

I would love to hear your thoughts, and your results achieved through this book. I look forward to hearing the stories of the impact it has had on your life. I encourage you to take up the free resources in the book that have been offered. If you want even more, then please reach out and connect with me on Facebook (**https://www.facebook.com/DrNatalieGreen**) or LinkedIn (**https://www.linkedin.com/in/natalie-green-36281918**) and I'll be more than happy to help you lead the life that you desire.

All the best, go out, shine like the diamond that you are. Thank you.

> *Go confidently in the direction of your dreams. Live the life you have imagined.*
> **Henry David Thoreau**

Appendix 1
Symptom Checklist

Be aware of what symptoms you have going on at present. If they have been around for a while, it might be worth considering that you need some assistance. This is by no means an exhaustive list, however.

- emotional withdrawal
- avoidance of reminders of the trauma that interferes with personal and work activities
- feelings of hopelessness
- self-destructive behaviour
- personality changes
- mood swings and changes in mood
- difficulty with sleep
- nightmares
- going over and over something in your mind
- fatigue and exhaustion
- difficulty concentrating
- irritability
- feeling unsure of yourself, having a lot of self-doubt
- overly perfectionistic and rule-bound,
- physical complaints such as headaches, stomach aches, upset tummy
- anxiety
- panic attacks
- sadness
- outbursts
- negativity
- aggression and agitation

- risk-taking behaviour that is unresponsive to correction and out of character
- change in eating or sleeping patterns
- change in appetite
- weight loss or gain without trying
- loss of previous control of bowel or bladder
- excessive worrying
- reaction out of proportion to an event
- changes in socialisation patterns such as withdrawal from friends and family
- preoccupation with stress
- worrying about what others think
- diminished interest in activities
- absences from work etc.
- nervous habits
- reduced self-care
- impatience and frustration with others
- substance abuse
- not going out anymore
- not getting things done at home or work
- feeling overwhelmed
- feeling irritable
- feeling guilty
- feeling ashamed
- being indecisive
- negative thinking
- constant rumination
- feeling sick and run-down
- racing heart
- tightening of the chest
- restlessness

- feeling on edge
- excessive fear or worry
- always thinking the worst
- avoidance of people or places that make you feel anxious
- poor memory
- self-blame for things
- feeling cut off from others
- being easily startled
- being 'on guard' or 'on edge'

Appendix 2
Life Change Index Scale (The Stress Test)

Event	Impact Score	My Score
Death of spouse	100	
Divorce	73	
Marital Separation	65	
Jail Term	63	
Death of close family member	63	
Personal injury or illness	53	
Marriage	50	
Fired at work	47	
Marital reconciliation	45	
Retirement	45	
Change in health of family member	44	
Pregnancy	40	
Sex difficulties	39	
Gain of a new family member	39	
Business readjustment	39	
Change in financial state	38	
Death of a close friend	37	
Change to a different line of work	36	
Change in number of arguments with spouse	35	
Mortgage over $20,000	31	

Appendix 2 – Life Change Index Scale (The Stress Test)

Foreclosure of mortgage or loan	30	
Change in responsibilities at work	29	
Son or daughter leaving home	29	
Trouble with in laws	29	
Outstanding personal achievement	28	
Spouse begins or stop work	26	
Begin or end school	26	
Change in living conditions	25	
Revisions of personal habits	24	
Trouble with boss	23	
Change in work hours or conditions	20	
Change in residence	20	
Change in schools	20	
Change in recreations	19	
Change in church activities	19	
Change in social activities	19	
Mortgage or loan less than $20,000	17	
Change in sleeping habits	16	
Change in number of family get-togethers	15	
Change in eating habits	15	
Vacation	13	
Christmas approaching	12	
Minor violation of the law	11	
Total		

Directions

If an event mentioned above has occurred in the past year, or is expected in the near future, copy the number in the score column. If the event has occurred or is expected to occur more than once, multiply this number by the frequency of the event.

Scoring The Life Change Index

The body is a finely tuned instrument that does not like surprises. Any sudden change creates stimuli which can affect the body, or the reordering of important routines that the body becomes used to, and can cause needless stress, throwing your whole physical being into turmoil.

Life Change Units
Likelihood of Illness In The Future

300+ percent	About 80
150–299 percent	About 50
less than 150	About 30 percent

The higher your life change score, the harder you have to work to get yourself back into a state of good health.

Holmes, T.H. & T.H. Rahe. *The Social Readjustment Rating Scale,* Journal of Psychosomatic Research, 11:213, 1967.

https://www.dartmouth.edu/~eap/library/lifechangestresstest.pdf

Appendix 3
Date Stamping Process

Date Stamping is a process that was developed by my very special friend and colleague, Margaret Johnson, who is a forensic psychologist specialising in the treatment of Post-Traumatic Stress Disorder (PTSD).

This was developed after years of working in the field with people suffering from severe PTSD and is a fabulous strategy that enables them to calm themselves down and take back control very quickly and easily.

As most of you will know, the brain is divided into two hemispheres (left and right). Each is responsible for different functions, as can be seen in the diagram overleaf.

The left brain is responsible for logical, analytical processes and is also the timekeeper, whereas the right brain is creative and emotional. We know that emotional memories are more laid down in the right brain and, when in there, cannot access the timekeeper.

The Date Stamping Process is simply used when a traumatic memory or emotion surfaces and may start to overwhelm you. It is recommended to do this so as to move it quickly from right brain into left brain where the experience of it can become more logical. This ensures that the next time the memory or distress occurs, the volume has been turned down on the emotional state and the person is calmed.

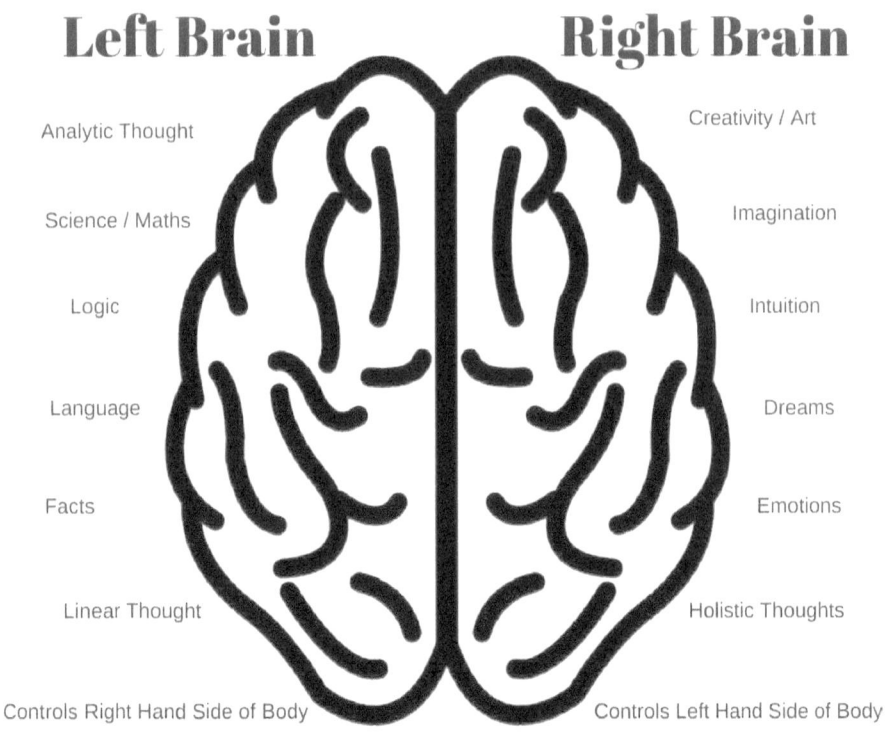

The Date Stamping Process

When the memory or emotion surfaces, simply say the following (you can say it to yourself or out loud):

'It is now [the date and the exact time] and I am in [the exact location] and I am safe'.

E.g. 'It is now Friday 10th March 2017 at 11:16 am and I am at home in my lounge room and I am safe.'

This process very cleverly integrates both right and left brain in a holistic and combined approach, and very quickly calms you down.

Appendix 4

Negative Energy Release and Permission to Move Forward Process

- Think about how you will feel when you become the new you. Now increase the feelings of excitement and satisfaction with who you've become.
- Who is someone whose feelings you are concerned about if you make those changes? Who do you not want to disempower in any way?
- We all have someone we're afraid of disempowering if we make these changes. It's a natural, normal thing, even though sometimes it can be tough to admit. It may be somebody who's not even alive anymore or someone who is alive and part of your life. It may be a parent, sibling, partner or mentor. Who do you think that might be for you? If you were to be completely honest, who is that person?
- What is the situation?
- What are you afraid of or concerned about?
- What is the underlying need for you? Love, security, recognition, value, status?
- What is the belief or statement that is driving/ motivating that need? (We often adopt these beliefs from someone else, often when we're very young, or we pick them up from past experiences. It's as if we enter into a silent or unconscious agreement that this belief is truth. This agreement becomes an obligation, almost like a debt we feel we owe, but are not conscious of).

- Who did you make this agreement with?
- Can you forgive yourself for that agreement?

It's time to give yourself a new power statement that serves the you that you are now and the new you that you are becoming. Your new statement is stated in the positive and begins with 'I am…' (e.g. 'I am strong and courageous and am in control of me.')

What is your new 'powerful you' statement? For example, a strong and courageous person who is in control of yourself, what is the action you will take and by when?

Now that you've given yourself permission to move forward, let's complete this transformation.

Appendix 5
Self-Care Practices

Unfortunately, many of us as humans are not great at engaging in self-care, especially on a regular basis. A lot of people see it as an indulgence or being selfish. However, I firmly believe that we *must* engage in regular self-care, even if only in short bursts to maintain our energy levels and ensure we are able to give to others as we wish to in life.

I love and completely agree with the saying: 'You can't pour from an empty vessel.' If you are run-down and exhausted, you have absolutely nothing left to give to others, let alone the capacity to look after yourself for even the very basics.

Here is a far from exclusive list of some basic self-care activities. I suggest you contract with yourself to choose at least one to commence as soon as possible.

- Relaxing in the bath
- Listen to a motivational CD
- Reading a book
- Setting and then revisit goals
- Going for a walk
- Sewing
- Doing some gardening
- Phoning friends
- Spending time with friends
- Watching a movie
- Exercising (walk or gym)
- Going to a concert

- Doing hobbies
- Going fishing, bushwalking etc
- Shopping
- Cleaning
- Spending time with family
- Playing sport
- Fun activities
- Looking at old photos
- Doing arts and crafts
- Doing Sudoku or crossword
- Listening to music
- Having time with pets

Appendix 6
The Negative Emotions Hierarchy

There are so many emotions that can be destructive, both to ourselves and to others. Here is a list of the various types of negative emotions that can slip in and take hold, especially if we experience things in our lives and hold onto them rather than looking to constructively work through them.

The strongest negative emotion is that of anger; as we move down the hierarchy of the emotions, they reduce in strength and power. Within each type of emotion, there are varying degrees of each type that you may be able to relate to.

Anger Emotions
- fury
- rage
- anger
- frustration
- indignant
- resentful
- cross
- annoyed
- irritated
- exasperated

Sadness Emotions
- grief
- desolate
- misery
- sorrow
- loss
- sadness
- upset
- lonely
- down
- blue

Fear Emotions
- terror
- petrified
- panic
- afraid
- fear
- anxiety
- apprehensive
- stressed
- nervous
- timid

Embarrassed Emotions
- shamed
- humiliated
- mortified
- disgraced
- exposed
- embarrassed
- shy
- self-conscious
- inhibited
- uncomfortable

Power Emotions
- despair
- helpless
- powerless
- depressed
- self-pity
- bored
- apathy
- jealous
- weak
- incapable

Guilt Emotions
- ashamed
- remorse
- guilt
- sorry
- blame (self-blame)
- regret
- distressed
- worried
- concerned
- troubled

Hurt Emotions
- hate
- hurt
- abandoned
- rejected
- offended
- disappointed
- disillusioned
- let down
- neglected
- vulnerable

References

Bandler, R. & Grinder, J. (1975). *The structure of magic I*. Palo Alto, California: Science and Behavior Books.

Bandler, R. & Grinder, J. (1976). *The structure of magic II*. Palo Alto, California: Science and Behavior Books.

Brown, B. (2012). *Daring greatly: how the courage to be vulnerable transforms the way we live, love, parent and lead*. New York, NY: Gotham Books.

Chomsky, N. (1964). *Current issues in linguistic theory*. The Hague: Mouton.

Crowley, M. (1999). *Self-esteem quadrants: new thoughts on a core issue in counselling practice* [online]. Psychotherapy in Australia, 5(4), pp 18–23.

Crowley, M. (2001). *Empowerment therapy, practitioner's manual*, 2nd ed. Tasmania 2001: Empowerment Corporation P/L.

Diagnostic and statistical manual of mental disorders, 5th ed. (2013). Arlington, VA: American Psychiatric Association.

Dilts, R. (2014). A brief history of logical levels. http://www.nlpu.com/Articles/LevelsSummary.htm

Dilts, R. et al. (1980). *Neuro linguistic programming: vol. I*. Cupertino, California: Meta Publications.

Dilts, R. (1983). *Roots of neuro-linguistic programming*. Cupertino, California: Meta Publications.

Doidge, N. (2007). *The brain that changes itself: stories of personal triumph from the frontiers of brain science*. New York, NY: Viking Press.

Higgins, E. T. (1987). *Self-discrepancy: a theory relating self and affect*, Psychological Review, 94(3), 319–340.

Holmes, T.H. & Rahe, T.H. (1967) T*he Social Readjustment Rating Scale, Journal of Psychosomatic Research.* 11:213.

James, T. & Woodsmall, W. (1988). *Time-line therapy and the basis of personality.* Cupertino, California: Meta Publications.

Johnson, M. (2000). *Date stamping process.* Orange, NSW: Forensic Psychologist of MJPS, located at 25 Prince St, Orange, NSW 2800.

Korzybsk, A. (1933) *Science and sanity.* Lakeville, Connecticut: The International Non-Aristotelian Library Publishing Company.

McKay, P. (2001). *Matrix therapies.* https://www.Evolvenow.com.au

Morrison, M. (2015). *Harvard-Yale written goals study: fact or fiction.* Peer Bulletin no. 255, December 1.

Oka, M. & Soosalu, G. (2012). *MBraining: Using Your Multiple Brains to Do Cool Stuff.* Timebinding Publications.

Pearson, S. & Haemmerle, A. (2012). *TCI Deep State Repatterning*, developed with attribution and contribution from Bandler, R., Grinder J., Robbins T., James, T. & McKay, P.

About The Author

Nat Green grew up in country New South Wales. She loved playing sport and always fostered a desire to learn, always striving to do and be her best. She is a down to earth 'country girl' and she always considered herself blessed with the upbringing and opportunities she was provided.

She went on to develop a professional career in the field of Clinical and Health Psychology. With a bachelor degree, a master's degree and a doctorate degree after over ten years of university training, as well as continual ongoing trainings and learnings, she has worked for over twenty-five years in the field of trauma.

She has always considered herself a trailblazer and a bit of a crusader. As a result she has dedicated herself to translating her years of experience into developing a revolutionary system – the ABS System – that will enable people to experience transformational change and free themselves of the hurts from the past that are holding them back, keeping them stuck and preventing them from living the life they deserve.

She has also experienced her own traumas first-hand which served to further drive her passion for developing and refining this ABS model even more. She has used it successfully with hundreds and hundreds of people in her practice and is now on a mission to take her model and share it with the world.

Ultimately she wants to make a bigger difference in the world and is now on a mission to inform therapists, clinicians and professionals about the ABS System and to embark on training them from a therapeutic standpoint so they can deliver the deeper transformations that the ABS model can provide one on one in their practices so more people can experience transformations and fewer people experience long-term suffering.

Nowadays, she lives with her husband and two children in beautiful Port Macquarie on the mid-north coast of NSW, which she feels is like combining her childhood country hometown with her own slice of paradise by the sea and enables her to have the best of both worlds.

'Transform Your Life' Online Course

Are you ready to take your experience of the ABS Model to a new level? Natalie has put together an online training course where you'll be taken through each of the seven steps with further tips, tools and strategies and practical implementation to move you forward in your journey.

This is your opportunity to get up close and personal with Natalie and to dig deep into each of the key areas that the ABS Model can be applied to across your life so you can really get the balance that you desire and create the life and the lifestyle you prefer.

The course has been divided into twelve separate modules so that you can take the recommended actions between each module and see the results from one session to the next.

Available to purchase here:

www.drnataliegreen.com.au/TransformYourLife

Dr Natalie Green as a guest speaker

Dr Natalie Green is a clinical psychologist, optimal mindset strategist and mentor who has specialised in the field of trauma and transformation.

She conducts lectures and keynote speeches from community to university level and has conducted workshops and webinar trainings on a broad range of topics.

Natalie understands how overwhelming life can be at times and thrives on helping people develop resilience and in challenging them not to settle for less than they are worth. She teaches on a range of subject areas in Personal Development, Health, Business and Learning.

Natalie is a sought-after guest speaker and can speak on any of the following topics:

- How to Use the ABS System
- Adjusting to Life with a Chronic Disease: for sufferers and carers
- Adjusting to Life with a Chronic Condition
- Grief and Loss
- How To Charge What You're Worth
- The Prosperous Therapist
- How To Run A Thriving Allied Health Practice
- Busting Through Your Money Beliefs
- Know Your Ideal Client
- Anxiety, Depression and Stress in the Workplace
- Caring For Yourself: the most important person in your child's life

Contact Information:

Mobile :- 0419 164 684

www.drnataliegreen.com.au

drnat@drnataliegreen.com.au

ABS Certification

Are you a professional therapist, counsellor or clinician that feels ready to break free from the constraints of past practices? Do you want to learn how to utilise the ABS system in your everyday practice and become certified in the delivery of the system one on one with your clients?

If you are dedicated to your clients and committed to excellence and want to pay it forward, and make a difference in others' lives, so that your clients can experience true transformations, letting go of their past hurts and creating the life they desire, I would be very interested in speaking with you further about how you too can become certified as an ABS Transformational Therapist.

We don't automatically take everyone through our certification; we have a very select application process. If you would like to be one of the select professionals to join me on my mission then please apply here:

www.drnataliegreen.com.au/ABSCertification

Additional Bonuses

For my Implementation Workbook Manual, go to:

www.drnataliegreen.com.au/ABSWorkbook

For other free links within the book:-

www.drnataliegreen.com.au/Letting Go

www.drnataliegreen.com.au/Forgiveness

ABS Transformational Workshops at discounted rates for purchasing the book:

www.drnataliegreen.com.au/ABSworkshops

1 day and 2 days, use Code: Diamond

Weekly Sanity Savers tips (free) (sign up at www.drnataliegreen.com.au/SanitySavers)

www.ingramcontent.com/pod-product-compliance
Lightning Source LLC
Chambersburg PA
CBHW021112080526
44587CB00010B/483